Jim Henderson brings us voices that orga̶ ̶ ̶ ̶ ̶ ̶ ̶ ̶ ̶ ̶ ̶ from those women who glory in their sub̶ ̶ ̶ ̶ ̶ ̶ become so alienated from the church that̶ ̶ ̶ ̶ ̶ it. While honoring them all, Jim asks the ̶ ̶ ̶ ̶ for anyone who wants to understand what̶ ̶ ̶ ̶ ̶ ̶ ̶ ̶ ̶ ̶ ̶ ̶ with women in the church today.

CHRISTINE WICKER, Author of *The Fall of the Evangelical Nation: The Surprising Crisis inside the Church*

A wake-up call to the church. Relentlessly straightforward, uncomfortably provocative, and unnervingly relevant. Don't read it if you don't want to be challenged.

TOSCA LEE, *New York Times* bestselling coauthor of *Forbidden*

In *The Resignation of Eve* Jim Henderson applies his incredible ability to ask good questions to a diverse group of Christian women. By framing questions in a unique and nonthreatening way, Jim enables us to discern what our sisters have to say about following Christ today, regardless of what we believe the Scripture teaches about women and the church.

JOHN H. ARMSTRONG, President of ACT 3; author of *Your Church Is Too Small*

The Resignation of Eve is sure to spark lively dialogue and clarify our own views on the role of women in the church, if we let it. Do we dare? We must! The future of Christ's beloved church, where each person should be empowered to use all of his or her gifts for building God's Kingdom, is at stake.

MARY SCHALLER, President, Q Place; author of *How to Start a Q Place*

The Resignation of Eve includes an amazing array of engaging stories from women, ranging from those who have stayed in traditional churches to those who have given up on church. There is a collective power to these diverse stories, as Jim invites us to reconsider "one of history's most radical advocates for women—Jesus of Nazareth."

DAN BRENNAN, Author of *Sacred Unions, Sacred Passions*

In his conversational style, Jim relates the unpredictable church experiences of more than a dozen women—and he challenges the church to listen to them too. The result is a profoundly honest survey of how women of faith relate to their own communities. Jim's thought-provoking conversation with these women taps into the previously unexplored territory of understanding why women engage with, or disengage from, their faith communities.

JENNIFER ROACH, Pastor of Light of Christ Anglican Church, Seattle

The Resignation of Eve is a valuable and right-on-time book for Christ followers. It helps define the tangled-up mess of gender and inequality that people of faith negotiate (or not) in the world of church. Jim Henderson has provided us a collection of multiple perspectives and experiences from the women he interviewed. Church leaders of all denominational persuasions would do well to lean in and listen with him.

PAM HOGEWEIDE, Blogger and author of *Unladylike: Resisting the Injustice of Inequality in the Church*

In *The Resignation of Eve*, Jim Henderson follows Christ in the revolutionary act of listening to women. That this is revolutionary already tells us much. Jim asks questions with a disarming frankness, and if we, too, listen to these women with an open mind, their stories will tell us so much more—not least the fact that it's probably later than we think.

MIKE HERTENSTEIN, Cornerstone Festival

When we stand before Jesus, all of us—women and men—will have to account for how we've invested the gifts God has entrusted to us. What are you doing with yours and those of the women in your life? *The Resignation of Eve* will challenge you to figure that out and act accordingly. Read this book, pray, ponder, and then do something.

ELISA MORGAN, President emerita, MOPS International; publisher, *FullFill*; author, *She Did What She Could*

the **resignation** of **eve**

WHAT IF ADAM'S RIB IS NO LONGER WILLING TO BE THE CHURCH'S BACKBONE?

jim henderson

BARNA

An Imprint of Tyndale House Publishers, Inc.

Visit Tyndale online at www.tyndale.com.

Visit Jim Henderson online at jimhendersonpresents.com.

TYNDALE is a registered trademark of Tyndale House Publishers, Inc.

Barna and the Barna logo are trademarks of George Barna.

BarnaBooks is an imprint of Tyndale House Publishers, Inc.

The Resignation of Eve: What If Adam's Rib Is No Longer Willing to Be the Church's Backbone?

Designed by Julie Chen

Published in association with the literary agency of Esther Fedorkevich, Fedd and Company Inc., PO Box 341973, Austin, TX 78734.

Library of Congress Cataloging-in-Publication Data

Henderson, Jim, date.
   The resignation of Eve : what if Adam's rib is no longer willing to be the church's backbone? / Jim Henderson.
      p. cm.
   Includes bibliographical references (p.   ).
   ISBN 978-1-4143-3730-2 (sc)
   1. Ordination of women—Protestant churches. 2. Women in church work—Protestant churches. I. Title.
   BV676.H45 2012
   277.3'083082—dc23   2011039939

Printed in the United States of America

18   17   16   15   14   13   12
7   6   5   4   3   2   1

Dedication

If I ever have to go to war, I want Pam Hogeweide by my side. She's smart, tough-minded, tenderhearted, and loyal. Pam has backed me up under extremely difficult circumstances and taken bullets that I deserved. She is a better writer than I'll ever be and selflessly advances others on her blog, *How God Messed Up My Religion*. Most of all, Pam loves Jesus and has dedicated her life to advocating and agitating on behalf of his favorite group of outsiders—women.

Contents

Foreword

FOR NEARLY FOUR DECADES I've been a pastor's wife and volunteer in a church community that believes the Holy Spirit distributes spiritual gifts irrespective of gender.[1] In practical terms, this means we believe it's possible for men to have spiritual gifts like hospitality and helps (which some consider "women's gifts"); and that it's possible for women to have gifts like teaching and leadership (which some consider "men's gifts"). It also means that many of the teachers and leaders in our children's ministry are men, while many of our senior leaders—elders, ministry directors, and teaching pastors—are women. To us, that seems normal.

As a church, we've often been criticized for our "position on women in leadership," but we've been criticized for so many things that I've learned to hold such criticism at a distance. Sometimes I even forget that our position on spiritual gifts and gender is fairly uncommon in evangelical circles. Reading *The Resignation of Eve* reminded me that this is still a hot debate and there are still smart, thoughtful, godly people lining up on opposing sides.

I have tended to avoid jumping into the debate because, frankly, it's not a personal issue for me. I never wanted to lead or teach, in the church or anywhere else. Seriously. When Bill and I started Willow Creek Community Church in 1975, I said to Bill, "I believe in this dream. I'll do anything I can to help make it happen. I'll clean toilets. I'll cook meals. I'll shake hands. I'll say private prayers. Just don't ask me to stand up in front of people! Don't ask me to teach! Don't ask me to lead!"

So I'm rather amused now when I look around a meeting room and realize I am the only woman seated at a table of ministry decision makers. Or the only woman speaking at a theological conference. Or when I speak out about an area of injustice and suddenly hear Christian women *and* men saying, "What can we do? How can we get involved? If you lead this effort, we'll follow you."

I wasn't aiming for any of this, not because of theological restrictions, but simply because I was terrified—of visibility, of failure, of disappointing people. I'm sixty years old, and it was only a decade ago that I finally quit kicking and scream-ing about my inadequacies long enough to hear the Holy Spirit calling me to live a bit more "out loud." In other words, I finally agreed to grow up and use my gifts, experiences, and platform for God's purposes. I still don't aspire to teach or lead, but if that's what it takes to live into God's calling, then so be it. I'll do my best.

During the last decade, I've traveled from Bosnia to Rwanda, from Lebanon to South Africa, from Egypt to the Democratic Republic of the Congo. In the devastation of disease and the horror of war, I've seen how messed up our world is. I've also seen God use amazing women to address the mess. You want to increase economic development in a poor community? Invest in microenterprise for women: about 98 percent of them will pay back the loan and they'll invest a full 90 percent of their revenue back into the common good (compared with 40 percent reinvestment by men).[2] You want to promote peaceful political and social change? Engage women in the process: they'll exhaust every possible nonviolent option rather than turn to violence. You want to end child marriage and assure that poor women have fewer but healthier babies? Educate little girls.

When women have half a chance, they change the world! I am convinced that women are our greatest untapped resource—in local communities and in the church. Unfortunately, I fear one of the unintended results of the debate about the role of women in the church is that some women fail to take themselves seriously. They don't think personal growth—stretching themselves intellectually, emotionally, and spiritually—really matters because, well, they're just women.

That's why I'm writing the foreword to this book. I doubt anything I've written will change the theological perspective of church leaders regarding women's roles in the church. But I do hope my words will encourage women—whatever their gifts and whatever church they're in—to take themselves seriously. Whether we're singing lullabies to babies (as I did last night to my six-day-old grandson) or protesting sexual exploitation (as I did recently at a forum on human trafficking), our voices matter.

The only thing more moving than hearing women cheer each other on is hearing a man cheer us on. Thank you, Jim, for recognizing Jesus' revolutionary love for women, for honoring women's stories, and for encouraging us to offer our full selves in service to God's healing, restoring, redemptive work in this world.

Lynne Hybels
OCTOBER 3, 2011

Preface

I THINK JIM HENDERSON IS a really fun guy, at least partly because he is a provocateur.

Not everyone is comfortable with that side of Jim. He loves to ask challenging questions, has no qualms about playing the role of "devil's advocate" in a dialogue, and gently but pointedly skewers simplistic answers. He enjoys taking sincere yet outlandish points of view seriously, and regularly offers some "outside the box" ideas of his own. He is willing to go the extra mile to discover genuine truth, justice, and compassion. Because he loves Jesus a whole lot, Jim does this mental teasing with a playfulness that is disarming.

It is this combination of qualities and practices that compelled Jim, against the better judgment of some of his friends, to write this book about the experience of women in America's Christian churches. Troubled by his observations of their plight, along with years of faith-related conversations with women from all walks of life, Jim became convinced that the roles typically assigned to women in churches are biblically indefensible, if not downright oppressive. True to his nature, he set out to address the wrongs, determined to improve the situation. In the process, which he continues in this book, Jim is making many people uncomfortable with the state of women in our nation's Christian churches—and, sometimes, with people's own beliefs about and behaviors toward women of faith.

Because he is a catalyst who enjoys substantive conversation, this book is filled with remnants of such exchanges about women's place in local churches. He uses these stories to raise important questions about roles, authority, love, responsibility, biblical authority, power, the essence of Christianity, leadership, church life, scriptural interpretation, and more. As you will see, while he is digging for understanding and truth, everything is fair game in his explorations and reflections.

The Resignation of Eve comes at a vulnerable moment in the history of the American church. At one point in his ruminations, Jim asks what would happen if female Christ followers en masse, all at once, simply stopped coming to churches, stopped serving others, and stopped delivering the leadership they provide. We may not have to wait long to learn the answer. Some of my recent research has revealed that women of faith, increasingly disgruntled and feeling unfulfilled by their church experiences, are already leaving churches in massive numbers. Here is what has happened between 1991 and 2011:

- There has been a 20 percent decrease in the percentage of adult women attending church services during any given week.
- There has been a 29 percent drop in the number of adult women attending Sunday school classes.
- The number of women who volunteer at a church during the course of a week has plummeted by 31 percent.
- The proportion of American women who are unchurched has nearly doubled in the past twenty years, rising by 94 percent. In fact, more than one-third of all women are no longer connected to a church.

In preparing to write this book, Jim not only talked to countless women across the nation—either in person or through online exchanges—but also commissioned The Barna Group to conduct a nationwide survey among women related to his hypotheses. You will find the results of that survey woven into the arguments made in this book. The provision of both qualitative anecdotes and statistical evidence makes for an interesting and thought-provoking read. (You'll find some of the data in tabular form in an appendix of this book.)

I don't know if I agree with all of Jim's conclusions, but I'll tell you this: he's making me think. I am grateful for that challenge. Sometimes it seems that those of us who are men in positions of church leadership don't think enough about the issues that Jim raises. It's good to be confronted on these matters. Grappling with the tough issues and complex situations of our faith is necessary if we are to reflect the heart of Jesus to the world. We are God's representatives of his love and truth; to represent him well, we must wrestle with such matters, no matter how uncomfortable they make us, or how much we discover we have to change our ways of thinking and acting.

Do yourself a favor; take your time working through this document. Clarify, in your own mind and heart, what you truly believe the Scriptures teach about power, gender roles, success, love, unity, and purpose. This is not fluffy stuff that you can blow through in an hour or two. Don't even try to do that. The questions raised in these pages are too important to give short shrift.

Jim Henderson: restless thinker, playful servant, man of God, provocateur. He wants you to join the conversation. It won't always be comfortable, but you'll be a better person for engaging in it.

George Barna
Ventura, California
August 2011

Author's Note

SINCE I SPEND A LOT OF time on airplanes, I'm frequently asked what I do. I decided to give myself a title that neither my fellow passengers nor I could completely understand (and that only a truly interested person would ask a follow-up question about). So I designated myself a "spiritual anthropologist."

I like this description for two reasons. First, a spiritual anthropologist sounds important, which I don't consider myself to be. It also gives me permission to be professionally nosy, which I am. I enjoy probing into people's spiritual lives and asking questions like "How do you navigate life spiritually—or not?" This anthropological impulse is what drew me into this project. I wanted to find out how women spiritually navigate the church and Christianity, particularly given the ferment in the culture and the church about women's roles.

While it was my own curiosity that pulled me into this undertaking, along the way it became apparent that a wider audience of Christians would benefit from doing some serious thinking about this issue, in light of realities like these:

1. Women are often the first leaders of vibrant spiritual movements.

   • Jesus chose Mary Magdalene to be the first human being to witness and announce his resurrection.
   • Women had key leadership roles in early Wesleyanism and Pentecostalism, the Salvation Army, and the American missionary movement.
   • In our own time, the growth of the Yoido Full Gospel Church in Seoul, South Korea, which in 2010 had 800,000 members, is attributed mainly to the leadership of women.[1] Women often lead underground churches, such as those in China, as well.

2. Researcher George Barna says women continue to be "the backbone of the church," even in churches where men hold most of the official leadership positions (pastor, elder).[2] In fact, some major denominations— and many independent churches—still officially limit the roles available to women.

   • Women are doing most of the work. Yet Barna has also found that they are more open than men to leaving their current faith communities.
   • In many families, women ensure their families get

to church. If the women leave, their husbands and children leave with them.

3. Regardless of anyone's theological persuasion regarding women, women can no longer be taken for granted by the church. Millions of Christians are reevaluating their spiritual options today. A majority of those Christians are women. Research shows that:

- There has been a significant increase in the percentage of women avoiding church in recent years. Between 1991 and 2003, the percentage of unchurched women rose from 18 to 30 percent.[3] In 2005, Gallup released a study reporting that 38 percent of women are unchurched.[4] A study by sociologists at the University of Nebraska–Lincoln found that although church attendance rates have been relatively steady over the past thirty years, "sizeable shifts have occurred within traditionally reliable churchgoing groups," including women.[5]
- Barna notes that women are more likely than men to reevaluate their spiritual options and, as a result, change churches, join a different faith, or practice their faith in new ways.

Songs emerge out of the interplay between music and lyrics; this book emerges out of the interplay between an observation and a question.

My observation: Jesus actively promoted women as spiritual influencers, yet women today are not given access to as much influence as they're capable of in the church.[6]

My question: How, then, do women perceive their role in the church, what are they doing about it, and what are the consequences for the church as a whole?

Who Do You Think You Are?

When I started talking to some of my women friends about *The Resignation of Eve*, they asked me who my coauthor was—meaning, "Which woman is writing this book with you?" They weren't the only ones doing the assuming. I normally work with coauthors, so I anticipated doing this book with a woman as well. However, early on it became clear to me that I was to write this book on my own.

I'm not surprised if some women misunderstand my decision or are even angry with me. By putting myself in this position, I'll inevitably be on the receiving end of a lot of frustration. But while I didn't have a coauthor, *The Resignation of Eve* wouldn't have been possible without the frank, heartfelt input of more than a dozen women. As readers of my other books know, I prefer to "get my preaching done through others," which is why I profile a number of women whom I've interviewed over the past year. I simply asked the questions, and they told their stories.

I present these accounts knowing that all of us operate under what I call *the myth of objectivity*. The myth of objectivity means we view ourselves as objective and those who disagree with us as subjective. The harsh reality is this: *when it comes to humans, there is no such thing as objectivity—only observations and opinions.* That is why I largely let the stories speak for themselves, even when the women profiled arrived at conclusions with which I personally disagreed. I approached the project this way because I needed to challenge my assumptions and biases about women and church. I needed to discover where my perception and reality clashed. In the process I not only learned about women and church, I also learned about myself. I hope that by the time you finish this book, you will be able to say the same.

—Jim Henderson

Introduction

PICTURE THIS.

It's 8:30 a.m.

You're in your office at New Life Community Church, getting ready to lead the ten o'clock service.

You hear some rumbling outside your study and make out the voice of Barry, your head usher. He's talking with a few other ushers who have arrived to straighten things up in the sanctuary.

You try not to worry about how many people will show up today. You turn your worries into prayer to help remind yourself why you do this.

Normally Linda, your longtime volunteer administrator, would be at church by now, busily inserting your fill-in-the-blank sermon outlines into the bulletins. You feel a slight flash of irritation at Linda's tardiness, but let it go since she's as faithful as the day is long. But it does seem unusual. You bury the thought and get back to your final sermon run-through.

The first notes from Sam's keyboard echo through the sanctuary, reminding you that you have about half an hour to finish your preparations. Sam and the other boys in the band—Frank on bass and Tommy on the drums—are getting ready for the sound check. These guys all played together in an eighties cover band until Frank got saved. Then they stopped playing the clubs, and Sam and Tommy followed Frank into your church. That was twenty-five years ago. Now they help lead worship every Sunday.

Billy, the twentysomething worship leader (with spiked hair), walks by looking perky and directs a quick wave your way. He's carrying his electric guitar and soon starts running through the worship set. "Lord, we lift your name on high; Lord, we love to sing your praises. . . ."

You think to yourself, *Not exactly the Time Warner worship band, but hey, the price is right.* Billy is interning with you while he completes his final year at Bible school. You know he's planning to apply for a music and arts director position at some megachurch. Knowing how tight the economy is and how ruthless church business can be, though, you don't anticipate losing him anytime soon.

It's closing in on 9:30, and you haven't heard a peep coming out of the Sunday school area downstairs in the basement. And where's Linda? Normally you'd ask your wife to fill in, but she's out of town caring for her ailing father. You start feeling that Sunday morning emotional mix (something between anger and anxiety) that pastors are very familiar with. You sense trouble.

You head out to the front lobby, doing your best not to appear flustered or un-pastor-like. That means you look unusually happy and shake hands more than a normal person would. Because your entire Sunday school is taught by women, the silence stuns you. There are no women anywhere.

A few dads with their sons in tow straggle in, the men desperately looking for their kids' teachers in the dark classrooms. Your throat tightens, fear turns to panic, anger turns to dread. You momentarily wonder if Hal Lindsay got the Rapture right but failed to mention that in the Greek it says *for women only*.

With no time for humor, you rush into the sanctuary, tossing furtive glances at the men who've figured out that there is no Sunday school. The committed ones are dragging their sons into the pews, where they expect you to explain why the good Lord told you to shut down Sunday school today.

As you head back out the doors leading from the sanctuary to the lobby, you stop to shake the hand of your church's finance chairman. "Hey, Rob," you say to the fortysomething man, who is pulling one boy by the hand and glancing back at the scowling teenage boy behind him. "Good to see you this morning. Hi, Tyler; hey, Robby." After a beat of silence, you smile and ask, "Umm, where's Susan this morning?"

Rob sighs and shrugs. "Wish I knew. After getting Tyler dressed, she told me to go on ahead; said she'd follow us later."

She's not the only one MIA, you think. *Where is Linda, anyway?* Your sermon outlines are missing from the bulletin, Sunday school is nonexistent, and the background singers are nowhere to be found.

Billy and the band forge ahead, trying their best to get the men and boys to sing the high notes. Collectively, their voices sound more like a moan than a melody.

Billy gives you "the nod," which translated means "Pastor, pleeeeaze rescue me from this incredibly awkward moment." Because you're the only person in the church who's paid to be a Christian, you do your duty. Walking up behind Billy, you touch his back like a tag team wrestler and begin to pray.

In midprayer, your cell phone rings. *You stupid dork*, you think to yourself, *Why didn't you turn the ringer off?* (Here's why—normally Linda reminds you of those details.) You clumsily grab for your phone, which is buried in the inside pocket of your suit coat. As you do, you notice all the other men doing the same thing, almost as if this moment had been choreographed.

"Pastor, Pastor? This is Linda! Can you put me on speaker-phone, please?" Not knowing what else to do and not wanting to appear controlling or angry, you hold the cell phone up to the mic on the pulpit. You briefly wonder if this is scriptural but being desperate decide this is not the time to split hairs. You want to know where all the women have gone.

You find your voice and composure. "Linda, where are you? And who's there with you?" You hear a lot of women chattering in the background on the other end of the line.

"Pastor, sorry for the interruption, but we ladies have been talking and praying about some of the needs of our church. We realized that we could help out with some of those needs—if we weren't limited in which of our gifts we're allowed to use around here. But rather than trying to get you to debate, we decided it would be more effective if we simply didn't show up one Sunday. We call it *Sisters Solidarity Sunday,* and we plan to do this kind of thing until you become comfortable opening up more opportunities for us to serve."

The men sit in stunned silence. They are used to their wives telling them what they think in private, but never in public—and never ever from the pulpit!

"Pastor, we don't want to interrupt the service. We can pick this up at our staff meeting later this week. You guys have a great time worshiping the Lord, and all of us women will do the same. See you!" *Click.*

"Linda? Linda?"

And with that, Linda finishes the first sermon ever given by a woman from behind the sacred pulpit of New Life Community Church.

If you think this scenario is a stretch, think again.

Write down the name of every woman who runs some part of your church (paid or volunteer).

Ask yourself what your church would look like if these women ever organized their own version of Sisters Solidarity Sunday.

This book is written to help you avoid that scenario.

CHAPTER 1

THE THREE FACES OF RESIGNATION

RESIGNATION IS ONE OF those fascinating words that can be used appropriately under opposite sets of circumstances.

It is used to express both resistance and acquiescence.

It can be used to express either outrage or submission.

When someone *resigns from a job*, it's the functional equivalent of saying "I quit."

When someone *resigns herself to a job*, it is the functional equivalent of saying "I accept."

Moreover, if I say, "I resigned from that job last March," I'm describing an *action*, but if I say, "I'm resigned to staying in the job one more year," I'm describing an attitude.

In the first scenario, I'm in charge; in the second, someone else is. If I quit, my circumstances are being shaped by me, but if I accept, I'm being shaped by my circumstances. Certainly, it's normal to do both things at different times. We have to. No one gets to do what he or she *wants* to do 100 percent of the time.

When we don't possess the freedom to change our work situation, we become resigned to it. Sometimes this doesn't even bother us, and we continue on, seemingly unaffected. Often, however, we "go through the motions" and appear to be present but in fact are not. We do the minimum needed to get by (and get paid) but do our most creative work somewhere else (often for no pay).

When we're dissatisfied at our workplace, we might quit or fire ourselves before we get fired. Or, on the other hand, instead of walking away, we might choose to remain engaged and work for change from within.

How does this relate to what I learned about how women are negotiating the church? All the women profiled in this book fit into one of the following categories:

- Some of the women have resigned themselves to their churches' positions on women;
- others have resigned from their churches because of those churches' positions on women;
- and, finally, some women have "re-signed"; that is, they've reengaged in their churches or in other churches, leading and influencing despite opposition.

So that you can get the most from these stories, let me offer a few more distinctives of each group.

Resigned To

In this book you will read the stories of women who have come to terms with the fact that they are not "allowed" to exercise all the gifts and abilities they're capable of contributing in the church setting. Some say they are perfectly fine with this reality. They've accepted the idea that the same people who deny them the right to lead their churches would go door to door on their behalf if they ran for president.

Other women love their churches and their people, but they know they aren't being given the opportunity to think, strategize, innovate, and create new ways of doing church that both men and women find appealing. Often when they have expressed their desire for more influence, they were blocked, stonewalled, or stalled. These women have acquiesced to the powers-that-be who are more than willing to allow them to run the operation but not lead it. As a result, many have lost the desire to be creative.

Resigned From

How would you feel if you were capable of leading, thinking, guiding, shaping, and forming a spiritual community but were denied the opportunity to do so? This experience leads some women to walk away from the church, Christianity, and in some cases God. That is the experience of the women profiled in this section. At one time these women were very dedicated Christians, churchgoers, and Bible study leaders, but they have since opted for other beliefs or no beliefs. Some maintain deeply spiritual, fulfilling lives but in a context that is separate from the churches they left.

Which is worse in your mind, *actually resigning* or *being resigned* to not being able to quit?

Re-Signed

We will look at one more type of resignation in this book—the *re-sign*. This is the decision some women make, knowing the limitations, knowing the risks, and knowing that things are not likely to change. Women who "re-sign" don't quit or accept things as they are; they engage, lead, and influence. They make waves *and stay connected*. They're engaged but not owned, integrated within the church but knowledgeable about its inherent limitations and dangers.

They're like those of us with extended family whom we would prefer to avoid but with whom we choose to stay connected. We do this for a variety of reasons—perhaps because they're all we've got. To Outsiders it may appear that we've "sold out," especially since they're the ones we often complain to about our unusual families. They can't figure out why we keep going back for more abuse each Christmas.

But we do go back—except we don't go back blindly or perhaps as often as we went at first. We are measured; we are in control. We're not going to get sucked completely back into the system that could suck the life right out of us. We don't expect these family members to provide our meaning, and we aren't surprised when they disappoint us.

Women who have re-signed either remain active in their

own churches even though they disagree with the churches' stances on women, or they intentionally plug into other churches that provide them with the opportunities they seek.

Women who have re-signed realize that life is a series of trade-offs. You don't always (or even often) get what you want or need, but you get something that provides enough meaning to make it worth the trade.

Women who have re-signed are realists and even optimists. They are willing to nudge the ball of change down the field. They're not world changers, but they're contributors. They belong to a long line of sisters and brothers in arms who are committed to seeing women be given equal opportunities to express, create, lead, and influence change inside and outside the church.

Women who have re-signed defend women who have quit and challenge women who have acquiesced. They advocate for both groups. They associate with both groups. They do not see themselves as having arrived and are never sure they are doing the right thing all of the time. They walk by faith, following in the footsteps of Jesus, who radically advocated for women in his time.

What Problem?

In those churches where women either acquiesce or leave, it can be easy to not even consider whether women are being given the opportunities God intends them to have. But if you want women to bring the best of their gifts and talents to your church, you need to know what they're thinking and saying behind closed doors. Here are the top four issues that emerged as I interviewed women for this book.

Doctrine

There's a lot of confusion among both men and women about what the Bible does or does not say about the role of women in the church. Women struggle (often in private) trying to determine whether their churches' positions on women's roles are genuinely God's ideal or simply a reflection of dogmatic conditioning and cultural bias. The most ardent students of the Bible on both sides tend to be the ones who are *most certain* their view of the biblical role of women is the correct one.

Given the polarization, I am dismayed at how uninterested Christians seem to be in trying to understand why their brothers and sisters can read the same biblical passages and come to opposite conclusions. We need to learn how to stay in the room with differences and not "break up" over every biblical disagreement. Frankly, I think this attitude needs to begin with pastors.

Disillusionment

Many women are discouraged. And while some of them, particularly young women, leave the organized church only, others walk away from the faith altogether. In fact, in 2010 The Barna Group found that 26 percent of Americans have changed faiths or adopted a significantly different faith view during their lifetimes. Barna released its study just after the author Anne Rice famously renounced Christianity on her Facebook page. According to Barna, Rice "shares a spiritual profile with nearly 60 million other adults nationwide," most of whom, the research found, are women. Since breaking with the Catholic church, Rice has publicly reaffirmed her commitment to Christ several times; however, Barna's report notes, "The most common type of spiritual shift was from those who were Christian, Protestant or Catholic in childhood to those who currently report being atheist, agnostic or some other faith. In total, this group represents about one out of every eight adults (12%), a category that might be described as ex-Christians."[1] Disillusionment with their church and religion was cited as one of the top reasons people gave for leaving their faith.

But for many women (particularly wives and mothers), leaving doesn't mean walking away; more often it means showing up without being present. Women often do this because they want their husbands and children to grow spiritually. They participate at the minimal levels and give just enough to ensure their families are included, even if the women themselves are not growing. They seem to be masters at finding ways to feed themselves without requiring as much from the place they call church.

Contradictions

It's been my experience that unless someone they love is directly affected, few Christians even consider whether the systems we've created in our churches reflect the same commitment to women that Jesus showed the women of his day.

Our denial that this issue even exists reflects the church's confusion. Many pastors (both conservative and liberal) say one thing in public (or more precisely at denominational meetings) and do something different in their own churches.

In later chapters you will read the stories of people who believe a woman can be the president of the United States but not the pastor of a church. You will also read about denominations that ordain women but still find ways to stop them from expanding their influence at the highest levels. If nothing else, these interviews will help you see that we Christians are one contradictory bunch. Hopefully the stories will provide you with insights as to how you might correct that habit in your own church.

Spiritual Brain Drain

Potentially the most serious loss the church faces because of this confusion is the *spiritual brain drain* of women. As you read these stories, you'll discover that when it comes to the spiritual development of themselves and their churches, women simply "outcare" most men. Some people seem to scold women for this, as if they need to cut back so as not to discourage men from taking their rightful place of leadership in the church. A few of the women I spoke with hear this as blaming the victim.

Certainly the pastor of the world's largest church, whom you'll read more about later, would agree. Pastor Cho of South Korea grew his church to close to 850,000 members by encouraging women to have as much influence as God gifted them with, and he did this in a culture that, unlike America's, has historically assumed women are subservient to men. Christian history may record that Pastor Cho's decision to open the doors of influence to women in his church was a primary contributing factor in his country's transformation from a predominantly Buddhist country to a Christian one.

We limit women to our own detriment, because they are not just good at caregiving and connecting, they're also good at strategizing, seeing patterns, and understanding what the long-term needs and objectives are. While not all women serving in our churches consider themselves leaders, many of them offer outstanding skill and vision and are energized by leading. While some of these women have either embraced leadership roles in their churches or prefer not to lead in church because they are so worn out from leading elsewhere, a significant number are frustrated because they can't lead at all or are not allowed to lead within their areas of giftedness.

And the Survey Says

As part of my due diligence for this project, I not only interviewed women, I also commissioned The Barna Group to survey a nationally representative sample of more than 600 women about all sorts of issues that affect them as churchgoers.

When asked to consider their churches' positions on women in leadership, the majority of the women voiced support for their churches' positions. Well over three-quarters said their churches' perspectives on women in ministry are either almost identical or similar to their own. Almost the same percentage said the senior pastors in their churches are somewhat, highly, or completely supportive of women leading in their churches. Nearly two-thirds said that all leadership roles in their churches are open to them.

What gives? If women in the church are as satisfied as they say they are, why are so many of them willingly considering bolting or switching churches? And why are more and more women, who as we noted earlier are the functional backbone of the church, staying away?

I found many of the survey results surprising, so I decided to prerelease a few of the statistics to the public to see how they would respond. The reactions were all over the place. Some women felt the stats were very accurate and questioned why I would want to analyze them further. They saw my attempt to drill into these statistics as another expression of the rejection of traditional roles for women.

Many other women, however, said the views shown in the survey once matched their own, but they have since reached different conclusions about women's roles in the church. Others went so far as to suggest that the statistics proved that women are afraid to tell the truth about their real feelings, not wanting to cast the church in a negative light.

Scattered throughout the book you will find pages called "Fast Facts." These highlight the survey statistics we prereleased, followed by some of the responses we received. It will become apparent that there is no consensus on these issues, but there are lots of opinions and much pain.

As you read the comments and the stories, I hope you'll spend more time pondering *how* you arrived at your beliefs about women's role in the church than you spend defending them.

Dual Data or Data Duel

This book, then, is the result of a unique data "mash up" of quantitative (statistical) and qualitative (story-based) research. In the world of research there's currently a battle going on between these two approaches. Think of it as mind share versus heart share.

In other words, the modern era gave us statistics and quantitative measurement. It also gave us the Internet, Google, and Wikipedia. As cultural sociologist Daniel Pink writes, "When facts become so widely available and instantly accessible, each one becomes less valuable. What begins to matter more is the ability to place these facts in *context* and to deliver them with *emotional impact*."[2] Pink is suggesting that when humans get information overload, they revert to stories. Interestingly, we modernists have been trained to value stats, but Jesus was more inclined to use stories.

Besides lacking the geek gene required to do the serious work of quantitative analysis, I am drawn to qualitative research by Jesus' example. As I see it, *stories are the new statistics.* Without question, there are limits to qualitative research. It's subjective, anecdotal, and at times difficult to verify. But quantitative research comes with its own baggage as well. It's overwhelming, sterile, and can often leave us trying to guess the agenda of the researcher.

Being the troublemaker that I am, I thought it would be interesting to combine the quantitative with the qualitative and let you draw your own conclusions from the picture that emerges. This is why my organization asked The Barna Group to partner with us.

One of the mantras public speakers recite to themselves as they take the stage is, *It's not what you say but what they hear.* The same could be said of statistical analysis. It's not what the research concludes but how you interpret it. *Statistical veracity lies in the eye of the beholder.*

Here's the deal: if you have a bias toward quantitative analysis, you will find more than enough statistical evidence to support your opinions. If on the other hand you lean toward qualitative analysis, you are likely to find the stories compelling, convincing, and moving.

What most of us are likely to do is simply toggle between the stats and the stories—hanging our opinion on a number here and a story there. Over time we create our own version of how things *really* are. Just remember what Anne Lamott said: "You can safely assume you've created God in your own image when it turns out that God hates all the same people you do."[3]

Bottom Line

George Barna summarized one of the findings of his quantitative research this way: "Among women whom the Barna

Group would classify as Born Again, few seem frustrated about their opportunities to lead in the church."[4] In fact, when asked how they felt about their role within the church, 61 percent said they believe they have much influence. That is even higher than the 55 percent of those not identified as Born Again who felt they had significant influence.

Depending upon who is doing the interpreting, Barna's conclusion could be (and without a doubt will be) read in one of three different ways:

1. Most Born Again women have no complaints about their role in their churches.
2. Most women have been persuaded to toe their churches' line on the issue of women's influence in the church.
3. When selecting a church, some women view leadership opportunities as a criterion, so it's not surprising that they landed in churches that reflect their views on this issue.

The same could be said (and without a doubt will be) of the conclusions I arrived at based on my qualitative research:

1. Some women are quite content at church.
2. Many women are disengaged and not able to bring their best to their church.

Understanding research, just like understanding the Bible, is all about correct interpretation of reliable data.

What I'm suggesting is that we need to start a new conversation about women and church. At the very least we need to think more honestly about these issues. All of us have room to grow and new things to discover about how God wants to use women to move his Kingdom forward. That's why we need to read, ponder, and think most deeply about the things we disagree with. Not to win but to learn. We need to *stop comparing our best with others' worst.* We need to stop criticizing each other and open our own ideas to critique.

Let me be crystal clear. My bias is that, just like men, women should have as much influence as they're capable of exercising in the church. But my opinion, regardless of how deeply held it may be, doesn't give me permission to ignore, dismiss, or demean those who disagree with me. And it especially doesn't give me an excuse to be mean. Jesus told us to love one another—not to agree with one another.

Most likely you have come to what you consider a well-reasoned and thoughtful position on what women should and shouldn't be allowed to do in church. This book is more of a pastoral appeal than a theological argument.

I want to invite you to take a closer look at the women who will be and are currently part of your church. I ask you to listen—really listen—to them. And more important, I ask you to consider the radical way Jesus related to women in a culture that sought to shut them down, curtail them, and control them.

CHAPTER 2

WHY IT MATTERS

Jesus didn't have favorites, but . . . he did *play* favorites.

At least that's the impression an uninitiated reader of the Bible could get. In general, Jesus seemed tough on Jewish insiders and soft on heathen outsiders. However, when it came to women—he basically liked them all.

Just think of the Samaritan woman; the foreign woman who begged for the crumbs off the table; the woman caught in the act of adultery; the woman who prostrated herself at his feet, kissing them and washing them with her tears before letting down her hair to dry them; Lazarus's sisters, Martha and Mary; the women who stood by him when he was crucified while the men hid; Mary Magdalene, to whom Jesus first appeared after the Resurrection. He seemed to be drawn to women's authenticity, loyalty, and openness to God, regardless of their beliefs or nonbeliefs.

What's interesting to me is that Jesus not only honored and protected women (a traditional role); he also provided them with a platform from which they could expand their influence (a countercultural role). As scriptural screenwriter-in-chief, the Holy Spirit chose to cast many women in the lead supporting actor role of the Gospel stories. This was because the star of the show (a.k.a. Jesus) was quite comfortable working with and alongside women.

It's a fact that Jesus did not choose a woman to be one of the Twelve, but it's just as true that he did not choose a man to be the first person to witness and announce his Resurrection. It's also a fact that no women were included in the inner circle of three who were present with him at Gethsemane and the Transfiguration, but it's just as true that no women followers bear the shame of having denied Jesus publicly.

Strong Women

I had to write this book.

I'm not sure about being called, but I do believe we can be compelled—pulled by an idea that *moves* us. Jesus called it the wind of the Spirit (see John 3:8). We *feel* the wind, but we don't know where it comes from or where it's going. Our hearts, like sails on a ship, are not designed to grasp the why and the where. Our hearts are designed to do one thing—respond. All we can do is raise the sails of our hearts and try to catch the wind of the Spirit. That's how I got involved in this story. I was carried into it.

The idea of speaking up for women has been rumbling around inside of me for decades. I grew up in a home with no men. My dad left home before I did, and Mom had to take over. She was strong and decisive, confident and playful. Mom led our little family of me and my three sisters from town to town, seeking new ways to survive. She never walked away from us, never abandoned her four little charges, and never took the easy way out. I jokingly tell people that if my mom hadn't been too proud to go on welfare we would have been better off financially. Instead, she worked herself to the bone and saw to it that we were fed, clothed, educated, and exposed to great music, creative people, and new ideas. She taught us to embrace the world—not to be afraid—not to limit ourselves. She also became an alcoholic, finally getting sober at age fifty-five. She recently celebrated her thirty-second year of sobriety. My mom, Jacqueline Wallace, is a great woman and a great leader.

I married someone very different from my mom yet very much the same. Barbara was a nun when we met. She was her dad's "hero." He always wanted to be a priest, but due to his unwillingness to be celibate and his desire to have a family, he was denied the opportunity to serve the Catholic church in that way. So Barb substituted for him. Fortunately, someone else had an even higher claim on her life. One afternoon, while she was staring out the big picture window of her convent, Jesus whispered four short words into her heart—*It's time to leave.* She had just one year remaining before she was to take her final vows.

By this time, she and I had gotten to know one another after some friends and I had struck up a conversation with her when we visited her convent. A few months after leaving the order, she told me about her experience and asked if I had ever considered marrying her (true story). I said yes, and one year later we were married. That was forty years, three kids, and two church plants ago.

Barbara is one strong woman. She is my muse and the only real home I've ever had. Barbara is the person I think with and learn from, and she embodies wisdom and practicality. If my idea gets past her screening process, I know it has a good chance in the marketplace. I should have listened to her when I was younger. I would have become a better leader, our children would have been happier, and we would have more money. But back then I was too proud and too sure of myself; besides, I was the man and a pastor, so I had God in my corner.

Barb had no desire for public ministry. My role as an evangelical pastor created untold pressure on her, and she eventually stopped attending church. She loves Jesus, but the typical church routine and mind-set made her crazy.

I remember Barb telling me, "If I get cancer, everyone will come to the hospital and pray for me and I'll be a hero, but if I simply (and honestly) say I need a break before I get cancer, I will be considered a sellout." Such is the state of Christianity today. It is safer to be part of a twelve-step group than a church.

It was a hard time for us, but I knew she was right and I backed her up. I had to come to terms with my own sense of inadequacy and eventually realized that as long as she was around and knew about church stuff—as long as I could process the goofiness with her—I was fine, but when she dropped out, I had to acknowledge that I didn't like the process much either. In many ways my wife was a forerunner of many more women I would meet along the way.

"You Tried . . . but You Failed"

Then there was Rose Madrid, a single mom with two preteen kids. Rose had felt called to ministry since she was a young woman. She had served faithfully in all sorts of roles. As a young Christian, she had emerged as a great helper to her pastor. Unfortunately one thing led to another and they had an affair. She eventually dropped out of church. A few years later, broken and divorced, she took a chance and started attending our church. Having found forgiveness and acceptance, she began to flourish spiritually. She became friends with Barb and me, as well as some other leaders, and became a leader herself.

At the time we were part of the Vineyard movement (soon to be denomination), and while there was no policy that explicitly forbade the ordination of women, no one we knew had actually done it. Yet her pastoral gifts were evident, and she eventually came on staff as my associate pastor.

When God gave me permission to resign, we ordained Rose as the senior pastor. Eventually Rose married a close friend who had lost his wife to cancer and who had been a pastor himself for thirty years. Today they copastor Vineyard Community Church in Shoreline, Washington, one of the most innovative churches in America.

Rose's courage (along with her husband Rich Swetman's support) made the way for her gift to flourish. Recently, in fact, Rose received her doctorate in ministry. Now numerous young women flock to her for advice, wisdom, and encouragement.

Rose is also a founding member of Off The Map, which Dave Richards and I started in 2000 to help the church see itself through the eyes of Outsiders.[1] Every year Off The Map presents at least one major conference to expose Christians to cutting-edge practitioners, missional leaders, and out-of-the-box thinkers. We specialize in bringing non-Christians on stage to tell us how it feels to be targeted and objectified by believers.

One of the things I discovered early on was that finding women to speak at our conferences was quite challenging. Frankly, there weren't many women whom our audience knew (translation: whom people would buy a ticket to hear).

Still, I prided myself on including women whenever I could. Rose helped me emcee the events, introduce other speakers, and lead prayers, but since no one knew her, I felt I couldn't give her a main stage shot. Following each conference we would gather the team together for a review.

I'll never forget what Rose said to me after one conference: "You tried . . . but you failed." She was challenging me to stick with my stated commitment to give women more opportunities to speak at Off The Map events, which she had every right to do.

I've read quite a few business books and learned that to be successful, leaders must seek the input/feedback/critique of their frontline workers. Using that analogy, when it came to women, Rose was my lead frontline worker—if I ignored her, whom *would* I listen to? The next year we committed to including and developing women as main stage presenters regardless of their marketability.

What's Worse?

Evangelicals are passionate about personal sin—swearing, adultery, gossip, drunkenness, lust, anger, and so on. They have significantly less interest in systemic sin—racism, greed, selfishness, and repression of women. We interpret the powers and principalities in high places that Paul refers to through a mystical rather than a practical lens. We pray against things but fail to protest them. This low view of systemic sin, this privileged paradigm of power, makes it easy for us to ignore the way we treat women in church.

We men compare ourselves with each other rather than with Jesus, which enables us to feel superior to many other men who are worse than we are. We operate like benevolent dictators who feel good because we allow a woman to think, talk, act, or serve and we don't treat them as badly as they could have been treated.

I recall once hearing Pulitzer Prize–winning journalist Thomas Friedman put it this way: "People who have power often don't think about it, but people who don't have power think about it all the time."[2]

Let me ask my male readers this question: when was the last time the word *allow* was used to describe what you could do in church for no other reason than that you are a man?

Christian women hear this message frequently, though it's often only implied. As a result, many women have resigned themselves to needing a man's permission to serve in a position of influence at church.

But this isn't the worst thing that's happened. The worst thing is even more insidious. The worst thing is that millions of women have given up protesting, given up trying to move forward, and allowed themselves to be convinced that they aren't and shouldn't want to be men's equals in the church that dares to name itself after one of history's most radical advocates for women—Jesus of Nazareth.

The worst thing is that millions of women have resigned.

Some women have resigned from Christianity, some have resigned from God, but many have simply developed a more insidious form of resignation, the invisible resignation that people develop when they've given up hope. This kind of resignation leads a woman to *appear* to be present when she actually left the building years ago.

This kind of resignation runs so deep that those who

practice it no longer even dream about a day when it will be different—they learned long ago that a dream usually turns out to be a mirage.

This is the resignation of Eve, and *it impacts the one group whose loyalty the church can least afford to lose.* The people who for the most part *run* the church, attend church, and pray and serve at significantly higher rates than their male counterparts.

Women.

Resigned To

Problem? What Problem?

Rose and Leigh are happy. One drives a truck for UPS, and the other regularly addresses women through a speaking ministry she cofounded. They both love Jesus, their husbands, their kids, and their churches. They can't understand how people can read the Bible and not see the importance of roles, hierarchy, and submission. For them it's all good!

Nancy was raised in a loving and vibrant missionary family. She married the love of her life— only to quickly realize her mistake. She absorbed her husband's insults and blows for years, but when he went after the kids, he crossed the line.

CHAPTER 3

SUBMITTED

The Rose Claxton Story

HER RETURN E-MAIL ADDRESS SAID "DOUG."

She even uses her husband's name on her e-mail account, I thought to myself. *Now that's submission!*

Not long after being introduced to Rose by e-mail, I had a chance to interview her by phone. It turned out that we shared a mutual interest in India. She travels there frequently to participate in the church-planting ministry of some mutual friends, which meant she already had my respect as a leader.

Rose began our conversation by telling me her story. As a wayward teen from a broken home, she got pregnant and got married, in that order, when she was seventeen. She and Doug weren't serving God at the time, but as the kids began arriving, she decided to go back home to what she had been raised in—the conservative evangelical church.

Twenty-six years and seven kids later, Rose and Doug faithfully attend a 5,000-member megachurch north of Houston. Doug works as a pipeline surveyor, and Rose drives a truck for UPS part time. Before that, she homeschooled all their kids until high school.

Rose is a hard worker, a trait she says she gets from her dad. Some of her early ambivalence about church may have come from him too. She says he was "the head of our home but struggled with measuring up in our legalistic church." For a time, she rebelled against the religion of her childhood. But Rose says her mom instilled Christian values in her, which eventually pulled her back to her roots. "You can't know the truth and walk away unless you are deceived." Rose spoke with a tone of certainty some evangelicals call assurance.

As a young mom, Rose bartended at night but took her kids to church in the morning so they could know the right way to live. Her first try at returning to the fold didn't go so well.

"I wanted my two-year-old in an older class, and they wanted him in the younger class," she says. "It seems goofy now, but it was important to me then, so I protested. Eventually the senior pastor and I got into it. Due to my childhood church experience, I was easily threatened by authority, which may explain what happened next. He suggested that maybe I try a different church. So I cussed him out and walked out of church with my kids. No one pursued me.

"A few months later I took my children to a large church in the Atlanta area—which is where we all began to grow spiritually," Rose says. "That's where I learned about the importance of women and submission."

Once she told me about her personal background, I explained that I was interviewing a number of women about their experiences with church and Christianity. My goal was to provide a candid look at how women feel about what they are and aren't allowed to do in the church. Before I could ask her any questions, though, Rose had a few for me.

- "How is your project helping the church?"
- "Aren't we focusing on the negative?"
- "I don't understand the purpose of this book."
- "If women get stirred up, how does it help the Kingdom of God?"

All fair questions, I said. I agreed that the issue of women's roles within the church stirs up deep feelings, but I believe as followers of Jesus we are obligated to listen to things we may not like but that are nonetheless important. When reasonable people hear how those with a different view arrived at their conclusion, it helps bridge the deep divide that separates them. I have observed that *when people like each other, the rules change.* As men and women hear the viewpoints of others who are not so different from them, all sides may move away from diatribe and closer to dialogue.

No matter where people come down on how much

influence women should have in the church, I said to Rose, everyone seems to agree that churches rely heavily on women.

"Really? How so, Jim?" she asked.

"Well, to answer that question, let me ask you a few questions," I said. "What percentage of the staff at your church are women?"

"Fifty percent," she said.

"How about Sunday school teachers?"

"Again 50 percent," she said.

And attendees?

"At least 60 percent."

"How many of them are elders?" I asked.

"Zero."

"How many of them preach on Sunday?"

"None. But, Jim, they sing on the worship team, and we do have women pastors who lead our children's and women's ministries. I don't believe women should be teaching men anyway."

I love this conversation—it gives me permission to probe the technicalities of a topic that's normally shrouded in mystery.

"So when do boys become 'men' so that women can no longer teach them?" I asked.

"I don't know, Jim. Around twelve, I think."

The *age of accountability*, which according to some church-culture traditions is indeed around age twelve, is treated with the reverence we generally reserve for Scripture. I've spoken with other women who explain that, in their churches, once boys reach the age of thirteen and are baptized, they can no longer receive instruction from a woman at church. (I'm not sure if the same rules apply at home.) This closely aligned with Rose's view of how the church should operate.

Although her name is Rose, she's no shrinking violet. It was her chance to turn up the heat, and she did.

"Jim, here's the deal. 'Women are more easily deceived than men,'" she said, paraphrasing part of 1 Timothy 2:14.

So I asked Rose if Paul's words in 1 Timothy 2:12, "I do not permit a woman to teach . . . a man," still apply today.

"Of course, Jim! I don't believe women should be teaching men. I don't understand how people can read the Bible and not see this!"

This is the theological rationale that informs the view of millions of conservative women today. These women are not thoughtless or mindless. They're convinced that the church and ultimately the world would be a better place if women saw the light and got in line with the way God designed things. Interestingly, many other religions, including Islam, hold a similar view.

Rose wasn't done. "Satan deceives women primarily through our emotions. Eve disobeyed God because she wanted authority."

She might have a point.

The emotional skills Rose accuses women of using to misappropriate authority seem to be creating an advantage for them as never before in the workplace. In an *Atlantic* magazine article titled "The End of Men," Hanna Rosin notes, "The attributes that are most valuable today—social intelligence, open communication, the ability to sit still and focus—are, at a minimum, not predominantly male."[1]

And yet Rose believes these characteristics are misdirected. "Jim, women are primarily the problem, *not men.* The boomer generation was so self-focused they didn't instill a value for family in young women. The culture of the sixties fostered this desire in women to find fulfillment outside the home. The church needs to call them back to loving their husbands and their children. Most young women don't have an older woman speaking into their lives like Paul instructed us in Titus 2.

"Usually when women hear *submission,* they feel like that gives them less worth, not more. Nothing could be further from the truth. I host a class called 'The Wife Class' where we have so much fun teaching women how to joyfully serve their husbands and family. We help women gain a whole new perspective and learn how to be grateful—how to stop being offended by their husbands and become honorable women of God.

"A woman recently grabbed me after class and said, 'My marriage has changed so much. I feel like I've found the key to the universe, but I need help to be accountable.'"

Then Rose put forward this unique proposal. "What if for one year women *were* silent? I think more men might stand up and take leadership."

I asked Rose if she was saying she thought men need to *man up.*

"I do, Jim! Here's something I learned early in my

marriage that touches on that: Doug and I had three boys and a girl close together. Lots of kids make for lots of opportunities to provide discipline, and I felt like Doug was being too harsh (not physically but emotionally). I would find myself trying to protect the kids from the wrath of Dad. After thinking about what I was learning about submission, I realized I needed to submit myself to his leadership. I decided to back off and stop usurping his authority. So when one of my kids would come to me with a complaint, I started telling them to obey their dad. I didn't feel like doing this—I made myself do this. When I did that, Doug became more reasonable with the kids—he changed.

"In fact, Doug came to me and said, 'All of a sudden I didn't have to overcome you.' Once I got out of the way and practiced being submissive, Doug stopped feeling like he had to fight me too."

I couldn't argue with her experience, so I switched gears and told her that I've been fascinated by the rise of Sarah Palin. Palin also attends a church that believes women should not teach or pastor men, yet she is a rock star to the women who attend those same churches.

So I asked her, "Rose, would you vote for Sarah?"

"No, I wouldn't vote for her because I think that's too much authority for a woman."

"So where do you draw the line?" I asked.

Rose launched into her well-reasoned defense of submission. "I believe authority is out of order when women are in leadership, whether they are the pastor or the president.

Women should not be in leadership in any of these roles. In fact, if Christians followed the Bible, we would give the world something to emulate, and more men would show up for these jobs."

Wanting to explore her logic, I asked the obvious. "So, Rose, let's say it's 2012, and Palin is running against Obama. Would you vote for Palin or Obama?"

There was a pause on the other end of the line.

"If the best conservatives can do is Palin, it would be disgraceful—they should find a man to run. *But* because I think it's our duty to vote—yes, if I had to choose between Palin and Obama, I would definitely vote for her."

What about Proverbs 31, I asked, which seems to encourage women to examine leadership in multiple spheres? "So should women ever hold positions of power?" I asked.

Rose recommends cautious deliberation in partnership with their husbands. "Jim, in order to answer that question, women need to consider the following:

- How is your marriage?
- Does your husband want you to be at home?
- Would he describe you as cranky?
- Who is teaching your kids to love and obey God?
- Do your children praise you?

"Whether you're a missionary, a day care worker, or the president of a company," she continued, "the key question for women is, 'Who's your spiritual covering?'² I know this sounds tough on women, but I think men actually carry a much bigger responsibility.

"And one final point, Jim. Submitting does not mean women are powerless. In fact I think *women have more influence than men.* God gave us this power, and if we accept his boundaries with a cheerful heart, then, as it says in Titus 2:10, 'they will make the teaching about God our Savior attractive in every way.' That's what I count on at home and at work."

• • •

My Take

I've no doubt that Rose's passionate commitment to a more traditional interpretation of submission is authentic. At the same time, none of us escape the influence of our past. When you consider her confusing childhood—the divorce of her Christian parents and her teenage pregnancy—it's easy to understand why Rose is grateful for the structure and security submission has provided for her.

Rose earned my respect for her sincerity, genuine love for Jesus and her family, and sacrificial love for the people of India. Clearly she is satisfied in her roles at home, work, and church. As our call came to an end, she told me, "Jim, I've never been happier or more fulfilled as a woman."

CHAPTER 4

TALL MEN DON'T, BUT I DO

The Leigh Gray Story

Few things fire Leigh Gray up more than studying the Bible and then teaching other women what she's learned. A few times each week, this thirtysomething mom of four records a brief devotional video blog, which she then posts at her website. Whether in a Gap sweatshirt and baseball cap or a fleece vest and houndstooth scarf, Leigh looks like any other carpooling mom as she sits with her open Bible to explain what God has been teaching her from a certain passage of Scripture. Leigh describes herself as "very outgoing," and that energy comes through in the way she looks directly into the camera and uses her hands to emphasize her main points.

I wasn't too surprised, then, when she brought up a

passage of Scripture during our first phone conversation. She told me she had just read John 20, the account of Jesus appearing first to Mary after he rose from the dead. I'd just finished reading about that passage in the book *Sacred Unions, Sacred Passions* by Dan Brennan. In his book, Dan makes the radical suggestion that, given the unique access granted to her by Jesus, Mary Magdalene could well be considered an apostle to the apostles.[1] When Leigh mentioned her interest in this passage, I was all ears.

"I was reading through John 20—thinking about the meaning of why Jesus would appear to Mary first," she said. "Then it hit me, he told Mary first because he knew women like to talk so much—Jesus knew she would run off and talk about it."

Leigh continued: "Jim, Mary went to the leaders first because it's a woman's role to defer to authority. She could have gone to her girlfriends, but she didn't—she went to the men."

I told her I was fascinated by the way Christians can read the same passage of Scripture and come to completely different convictions about its meaning. To better understand where Leigh was coming from as she read Scripture, I asked her about her spiritual background.

Leigh told me that she accepted Jesus as her personal Savior at the age of eight in vacation Bible school. "I never really slipped away—didn't drink or do drugs." Her mom and dad reinforced traditional marital roles. "If we asked Mom for permission to do something, she would always tell us, 'Go ask your dad,' something Clay and I continue to practice with our kids as well." Leigh and Clay met at a Christian university, where she double majored in psychology and physical education.

In 2006, she cofounded Speaking Thru Me Ministries, which provides women speakers for churches and conferences without charging a fixed fee. The organization explained the goal of one of its recent conferences this way: "The time of Christ's return is closer than it has ever been before, and yet it seems that people are driven further and further from the church for various reasons. Here is a way to bridge the gap! *This conference provides an opportunity for a wife to get her husband to a Christian event . . .*" (emphasis added). Leigh explained that she and her team of five other speakers teach women how to help their husbands grow spiritually without usurping the men's authority.

Before moving to their current home in Carmi, Illinois, Leigh and Clay attended a large evangelical church in North Carolina, a church of almost twenty thousand at the time. "I worked at the church as its health fitness director—teaching aerobics, volleyball, cheerleading, weight training, and bitty basketball."

"Biddy basketball?" I asked.

"Not basketball for old biddies, Jim; basketball for little kids."

Churches like the one in North Carolina are virtual cities unto themselves, which is one reason Leigh and Clay were happy to take a job change a few years ago that required a move to the Midwest. "The aerobics classes had become a church-members-only kind of thing—a little too ingrown for us—kind of like a Christian club."

Having spent a couple of years living in the Midwest myself, I was curious whether Leigh experienced any kind of cultural shift as a result of this move and, if so, how that affected her ministry experience.

"In North Carolina, I rarely spoke to mixed audiences," she said.

"What's a mixed audience?" I asked. "Interracial?"

"No, Jim—men and women. When we moved to the Midwest, the opportunities to speak increased, but many of them were to mixed audiences, which I found confusing. I had to really seek the Lord and the Scriptures to determine if I was supposed to take these opportunities or not."

Throughout our discussion, Leigh's enthusiasm and charming accent were infectious. But she became increasingly reflective as she began talking about her experience as a woman trying to make sense out of "her call" and "her culture."

"Ultimately I decided that as long as I wasn't usurping the pastor's authority or the direction he was setting for the congregation, I could minister to a mixed audience," she said. "I trusted that if my being there offended the men, the pastor wouldn't have invited me in the first place."

The scriptural rationale for Leigh's emotional dilemma is found in 1 Timothy 2:12, where the apostle Paul tells the church, "I do not permit a woman to teach or to have authority over a man; she must be silent."

Taken at face value, this Scripture clearly forbids Leigh

from speaking to any mixed audience ever. "So, Leigh, do you think Paul was just talking to this particular church about their particular problems—what some call a cultural application?"

"Jim, you do have to look back at the cultural setting. Women were talking too much—looking for attention—trying to be over and above the men in authority whom God had placed there."

Leigh explained how she differentiated between pastoral authority and scriptural authority.

"Like I said earlier, Jim, after praying about it and getting counsel, I decided the important thing was that I never usurp a man's authority—that's the kind of authority I think Paul is addressing here. So as long as that man or pastor is allowing me to speak, then I have a green light to deliver the message."

Her reasoning sounded a little convoluted to me, I told her, but since I know we all practice some version of Bible cherry-picking, I relented—almost.

"Hey, Leigh," I said, "one more question. What about that passage in 1 Corinthians 11:10-13[2] where Paul instructs women to cover their heads as a sign that they are submitted to the authority of their husbands? There are some deeply devoted followers of Jesus in the Amish and Anabaptist traditions who still practice this. You seem very committed to the idea of your husband being your covering; why don't you wear a scarf like the Amish?"

"I think Jesus freed us from cultural expectations like that. Didn't he, Jim?"

"So it doesn't apply today?"

"I don't think so. I take my cue from Beth Moore and Kay Arthur," she said, "two powerful women teachers from the evangelical tradition who speak to mixed audiences. Those women never attempt to exercise pastoral authority—they simply teach the Bible."

"Kind of like Paula White and Joyce Meyer?" I asked.

Leigh was silent for a long moment. "Well, not exactly, Jim. Beth and Kay would never compromise."

"Compromise, Leigh?"

"Well, I think that both Paula and Joyce are pastors; aren't they, Jim?"

"So they're doing the same thing as Kay and Beth, but because they're also pastors they're out of order?"

"Jim, I don't believe that women should be elders or deacons or anything that encourages men not to take the lead in church. As I see it, 90 percent of the time a woman takes a leadership position, it will look demeaning to a man. In fact, it really bothers me when a woman even wants to take the offering because it's just another authority thing."

"So it's the woman's fault that men don't lead?" I asked. "Sounds very similar to Adam's 'the woman you gave me' blame-shifting attempt in Genesis."

Leigh was experiencing a mix of emotions as she tried to explain how she navigates the complex world called church from the viewpoint of a gifted woman speaker.

"It's not just men," she said. "Women are even more complicated."

I'd heard this "some of my worst friends are women"

lament from several other women I'd interviewed, so I asked Leigh to elaborate.

"Jim, I'm a tall woman—almost six feet. Added to that, I'm loud and confident, so when I walk into a room I attract attention. When I walk on a stage, it's even worse. I take extra precaution to come across with humility—being a woman, I have a steeper hill to climb. What I've discovered is that while tall men instill confidence, tall women intimidate! A man can be confident and get away with it, but other women can't handle a confident woman. Unfortunately, they often couch their jealousy in Bible talk, like the time I was told by a woman that I was 'doing everything for my own glory.'"

My heart broke for her. Leigh is the same age as my daughter Sarah, so I wanted to reach out through the cell phone and give her a hug.

Ever the soldier for Jesus, she marched on. She pointed out one way her denomination tries to maintain the distinction between God's calling on men and women. "In our church tradition, men are called ministers but women are called directors. They can do the exact same ministry but must have different titles because men can be ordained but women can't."

It sounded strange to me, but not to her.

"Does this work for you, Leigh?" I asked.

"Sure, Jim!"

Needing to take advantage of my limited time on the phone and at the risk of being abrupt, I shifted the question to an issue I know conservative Christians feel passionate about—the negative influence of liberal culture as it began emerging in the sixties (more specifically, some of its outcomes, such as the pill, pot, abortion, and feminism). This conviction fuels much of the passion around politics, and I suspect influences the way women have come to view the issue of submission.

I asked this Gen-X mother of four if she agreed that the cultural drift to the left had negatively influenced gender roles.

"Definitely, Jim. I think that culture has made men weak. They've lost the authority they once had in the fifties during the *Leave It to Beaver* era. Just compare the men in today's sitcoms with Ward Cleaver. He was a man's man—the head of the home and an authority figure. Today we have shows like *Two and a Half Men* that picture dads as losers. They suggest that anyone can be a dad and that the kids are the smart ones."

So do you think feminism is to blame for this emasculation of men?

"Well, when it comes to the church, I think if there hadn't been such a rise of female speakers, maybe more men would be leading. I admit I'm sometimes not sure myself that God intended for me to be doing what I'm doing. Like the Bible says, everything is permissible, but not everything is beneficial [referring to 1 Corinthians 6:12]."

Since more conservative Christian women are running for public office, I was curious how Leigh felt about the prospect of a woman president. "How about outside the church,

Leigh?" I asked. "Can a woman lead, have influence over men, and become . . . say . . . the president of the United States?"

I was curious about her views on a woman president because there's a difference of opinion in conservative ranks over this issue. Purists say women cannot lead in the church or out of it, but pragmatists believe women can lead in any capacity *except the church*. Leigh turned out to be a purist.

"I don't think a woman should ever have authority over a man. When women lead, it demotivates men from becoming what they're supposed to be. God has given a man certain qualities. He is the one God has equipped for leadership. Putting a woman in leadership over him is almost like whipping him."

"So does that mean you would vote for Obama over Palin?"

"Noooooo, don't ask me that, Jim. Well, since it's our duty to vote, yes, I'd have to vote for Palin," she said.

"Better the devil you know . . . huh?"

"I guess so."

• • •

My Take

In his seminal book To Change the World, *James D. Hunter says, "It is not an exaggeration to say that the dominant public witness of the Christian churches in America since the early 1980s has been a political witness."[3] Over the past thirty years, the church has devoted the best of its public witness to political involvement. In my conversations with young people, this is one of the top three complaints they have about Christians.[4] Christians no longer divide over denominations; they divide over politics.*

This prioritization of politics is reflected in Leigh's dilemma. She truly believes that it's unbiblical for a woman to lead men, even going so far as to imply that such behavior is equivalent to "whipping" a man. Nevertheless, her dedication to this biblical principle is overshadowed by a higher commitment to her learned political principles. When I made her choose, she figuratively held her nose and stated that in spite of her deeply held belief that a woman should never lead a man, it was better that a conservative Christian woman lead our country than a liberal Christian man. Leigh preferred to take her chances on the devil she knew rather than the one she didn't know. I think we all do that at one time or another.

CHAPTER 5

YOUR LIFE WILL NEVER BE THE SAME

The Nancy Murphy Story

UH OH. . . . How did I get stuck in this group?

As the talking stick slowly circled its way toward me, all I could think was, *I'm not going to cry.* Our instructor had told each one of us to "tell our story" when the talking stick reached us.

As someone who's paid to be a Christian, I've learned the skill of appearing to be transparent without being vulnerable. Fortunately, this time I failed. As my hand gripped the stick, the tears began to flow. My hidden pain found words. My knee-jerk inclination to appear strong broke and my emotions took over. All because of Nancy.

Nancy Murphy is the executive director of Northwest

Family Life, an agency dedicated to helping the victims and perpetrators of domestic violence. This particular day, she was the visiting professor at Bakke Graduate University, where I was studying for my doctorate in ministry.

The talking stick wasn't a gimmick; it was a part of Nancy's life. The daughter of missionaries, she grew up among the First Nations Indians of Canada. Nancy's earliest memories are of sailing along the shores of Vancouver Island presenting the message of Jesus to the last, the least, and the marginalized.

"I thought I was First Nations till I was eight years old," she told me. "My dad's missionary work began when he was just nineteen aboard a fifty-foot wooden vessel that was traveling the coastal waters of British Columbia. Along with one or two others, my father traveled into every nook and cranny of the coastline to bring the gospel of healing and redemption to loggers, fishermen, lighthouse keepers, First Nations people, and hermits. Blowing his trumpet as the boat came ashore, my father would always attract a crowd. He playfully invited the men to arm wrestle, box, or try beating him at running broad jump. He struck a deal that if he won, they would agree to come to church that day. If he lost, it was their choice.

"My dad loved to sing, tease, eat, and help others in any way he could. He married my mum, a registered nurse and a woman with much more class than he. She was raised in the city, and though this rugged lifestyle was new to her, she loved the adventure and the relationships with the people of the coast. I was born within their first year of marriage, and two years later she gave birth to twins, a boy and a girl."

At age eighteen Nancy headed off for college at Trinity Western in Vancouver. Her rustic missionary upbringing had exposed her to many adventures with sinners, but now she was going to learn more about the saints—they could be compassionate, complicated, and dangerous.

"Those were the Jesus people days, so naturally as a dedicated Christian I got involved running a coffeehouse for Christ. That's where I met the man who would become my first husband. He was strong, handsome, and full of adventure. His shoulders were broad and his arms were strong. He had a passionate faith in Jesus, read his Bible with fervor, and was lots of fun. He'd had one of those Nicky Cruz conversions I'd read about in *The Cross and the Switchblade*. He and I married and planned to live and work among the poor in downtown Vancouver after our honeymoon.

"I was so excited to be starting my life with this strong man whom God had miraculously saved and brought into my life. On the third day of our honeymoon we went to the home of some close family friends who had lent us their beautiful house."

As I mentioned, Nancy works with victims of domestic violence. Little did she know that she was just about to begin her own painful journey into that world.

"I woke up early in the morning after having had a really bad dream. I dreamt my husband was having sex with a friend of mine. I felt dirty and wanted to get it off my mind, so I told him I needed to pray. Surprisingly *he told me* to stay in bed. I was a bit taken aback by his sharp tone, but I went outside anyway. As I was praying, he came up from behind and began hitting me and swearing at me. I'd never heard him talk or act this way. I was shocked. I yanked my wedding ring off and threw it down on the beach. That prompted him to yank his ring off and throw it and his little pocket New Testament into the ocean. That's when he said, 'Your life is never going to be the same again.' He was right; everything changed."

Nancy, of course, had been trained in the evangelical way and understood what Scripture said about divorce. "The parts of the Scriptures I knew about wives and marriage read like this: 'Wives, likewise, be submissive to your own husbands, that even if some do not obey the word, they, without a word, may be won by the conduct of their wives, when they observe your chaste conduct' (1 Peter 3:1-2, NKJV)." She pointed out to me that this passage was preceded by reminders from the apostle Peter about Jesus' willingness to suffer unto death.

"I mentally recounted my wedding vows," Nancy continued. "What had I committed to? 'I take you to be my lawful wedded husband, for richer, for poorer, in sickness and in health 'til death parts us.'

"Well, I wasn't dead, so it sounded as if *it was my job* to adjust my behavior to 'win' my husband. This type of behavior was all new to me. I was totally unaware that violence could exist in a marriage where both were Christians.

"I didn't have more than two or three minutes before the

violence escalated, and I had to make a quick choice. I had just married a man I loved. It was just the two of us . . . alone, finally. We'd already made love. I felt as if I had no other choice. I turned to him and said, 'I'm sorry.' I told him I wouldn't 'disobey' him again, and I begged him to calm down. He did. He explained that *I had done something* that had caused him to hit me. I'd left the room when he'd told me not to. I promised never to do that again, and I felt a big piece of my heart shrivel to the size of a dried pea. It had been so large just the day before. That was over now."

Nancy spent the next ten years attempting to *win* her husband—to help him stop hitting her. On one particularly heart-wrenching night, Nancy and her husband were staying with their pastor and his wife because they were in the midst of moving. Late that evening, her husband left the house and didn't return until the wee hours. He told Nancy he'd picked up a hitchhiker and then had sex with the woman because Nancy "didn't seem to have any time to talk" with him anymore.

Turning to her hosts for support, Nancy told the pastor's wife about her husband's abuse. This woman suggested that perhaps this was happening because *the two of them weren't faithfully attending church* like they used to. Nancy was speechless. She didn't want to explain how terrible Sunday mornings were; how she'd get ready for church, only to have her husband turn on her—slapping her, swearing and calling her names. In the end, they rarely made it to church.

As Nancy was pouring out her heart to the pastor's wife

that morning, the pastor had taken Nancy's husband out to run errands with him, and Nancy hoped perhaps he would see the seriousness of the situation.

Instead, when they returned home, the pastor took Nancy aside. He told her that he knew her husband had treated her terribly the night before. Then he added, "But I've spent the whole day with him, and he's a really special guy! I'm wondering what you would think if I asked him to *be my assistant pastor* after this has all been worked out?"

Nancy couldn't believe it. "These were dark nights of the soul. I was completely isolated from friends and family, in a sham marriage pretending we had a real marriage because we all know that God hates divorce."

Later, she tried confiding in yet another friend, who was married to a well-known evangelist in the area, only to hear that this woman had it even worse in her own marriage. "I walked away from that conversation feeling more trapped than ever. What kind of a crazy religion had I gotten myself into where even my role models were living a double life?"

As I listened to Nancy, I could barely constrain myself. How had she been able to stay with this creep for so long? Nevertheless, Nancy kept trying to "win" him over. All that changed, though, when she saw him kick their youngest child down a long hallway, leaving him alone to cry and restraining Nancy when she went to pick up and comfort her son.

"It was right there and then," she says, "that I determined to walk away from the kind of Christianity that had brain-washed me into thinking that this was acceptable behavior.

I had absorbed his blows, but my children wouldn't. I was going to do whatever I had to do to protect them. I couldn't see how a dead child could accomplish the purposes of God, and if it did, I would rather die and go straight to hell than follow such a ridiculous God. I was an utter failure at 'winning' my husband."

With the help of a pastor, Nancy and her kids looked for refuge. She had no resources and was completely dependent upon the kindness of the Christians, who could be harmful or helpful, depending on the day. Fortunately this time Nancy found a follower of Jesus who had ears to hear and eyes to see what was really going on with her.

"I asked a longtime friend of my brother's if I could talk to him. I decided to bring him an apple pie, hoping to soften the impact of hearing my story. He took the pie, but held it in his hands for the entire three hours it took for me to pour out my story. He did not take one bite. When I was finished, he put the pie down and I braced myself. Given the abuse I'd become accustomed to, I was prepared for him to hit me. I held my breath and tightened my grip on the seat of the chair. He leaned forward and said softly, 'Nancy, I'm so sorry. I had no idea.' I asked him if he was going to hit me. He shook his head and whispered, 'I would never hit you, Nancy. Your husband had no right to hit you, and I'm going to help you get away from him.'

"I was shocked—dumbfounded—completely drained of emotion," Nancy said. "I went to bed that night exhausted from years of living up to the commands I'd learned to obey:

'Don't fold my pants with a crease down the middle.'

'Always have a chocolate cake ready for me in case
    I'm hungry.'

'Don't ever ask me where I'm going or when I'm
    coming back.'

'Take the car only when I say you can.'

'Do not move when I'm talking to you.'

'Put the kids to bed before I get home from work.'

'Keep the house clean.'

'Don't have friends over unless I give you permission.'

'Don't dress like you shop from the mission barrel.'

"Over the years I'd lost my stamina to resist. I had completely acquiesced. Now I was disobeying, *making a decision
without my husband.* This surely would rouse the sleeping
giant. I experienced a fear I had not previously known. In
trying to escape—find a bit of rest and free space for my
children, I'd set in motion something far more serious. I slept
fitfully that night."

Nancy's brother's friend came by early the next morning
and helped her move her things to his sister's house, where
she and her kids spent a few happy and secure weeks. "Her
kind acceptance of our little family," says Nancy, "brought
back wonderful memories of my youth. There was a park
nearby. We laughed and played, ran and hugged. We were
free! We were happy! And, most of all, we were alive!

"We had no money and were dependent on the generosity
of our hostess, who proved to be a delight. She suggested that

I see a Christian counselor friend, which I did to be polite. He proved to be compassionate and well-meaning, but naive. In the final analysis he suggested that I try and reconcile with my husband one more time, which I reluctantly agreed to do. Only this time I told my husband if he ever hit me again I would be gone forever. He, of course, swore he would never do that. He was repentant—again."

Not long after, he made a disparaging comment about some close friends while they were driving to church. She gave him a look, and he slapped her face. "For me, that was the end," says Nancy. "It took several more months to find a way, but in that moment, I determined to leave him.

"I was eventually granted a legal separation. Being a Christian, I still didn't want a divorce; I just wanted the craziness to stop. During this time my husband never attempted to see the kids, but periodically he would break into my house at night demanding sex, saying, 'You're still my wife—so I have the right.'"

Using a network of friends who formed something akin to their own underground railroad for her, Nancy and her three kids made their way south to Seattle, where she would recover an important piece of life she'd lost.

Some young Christians took Nancy and her kids in, telling her that their religion was worthless if they ignored the plight of the widows and orphans. The safety and community of care they provided was significant, but Nancy continued to miss her life back in Canada.

"I longed to return to Canada and to all that was familiar

to me. By then, the sleeping giant, my ex-husband, had been roused. I had taken his children—whom up until then he'd seemed to show so little interest in—away from him. His family was outraged. Old friends began to call and write letters condemning me for leaving and for divorcing, and suggesting they would offer forgiveness if I would return. My ex-husband *had changed*, and they were supporting him.

"I almost went back to him. There were days I would rather die than return. Other days I'd rather return than live. I had no money, no family close by, no familiar support system, and no way to locate a God who wasn't so condemning. I particularly hated the fact that I needed a 'scriptural reason' to feel free. I hated that I wasn't strong enough to 'get over' all the other women I knew he'd had sex with while we were married. I hated that I wasn't good enough for my husband. I felt weak."

Meanwhile, Nancy excelled at the university. After so many years of verbal, emotional, and physical abuse, Nancy assumed she'd received As not because she was actually smart but because her professors *felt sorry for her*. Seattle Pacific University has a mission to equip students to serve others, so Nancy ended up being exposed to a whole new kind of Christian thought, and slowly became free from the toxic "faith" of her marriage.

"In one of my classes, an advocate who worked at a battered women's shelter came to speak about the continuum of violence. She told us that physical abuse starts off with minor expressions such as pinching, squeezing, and even tickling, but over time grows in intensity and severity. Sometimes, she said, it led to death by murder or suicide.

"At the end of her talk, I held up my hand and said, 'All those things happened to me, except for the murder/suicide, and *I'm not a battered woman.*' A big tear dropped down the face of the presenter. 'All those things happened to you? I'm so sorry.' She invited me out for lunch, and I agreed to go because I knew that I was *not* a battered woman. *I was just a woman who couldn't get things right.*

"At lunch, she grabbed a napkin and on the back began to draw what she called the cycle of violence. Tension that leads to an explosion that leads to a honeymoon of sorts with all sorts of apologies, promises, and even tears but eventually leads to tension again. Suddenly my experience made sense. The tears my husband had shed on our honeymoon were not tears of repentance but the tears of an unrepentant abuser, part of the cycle."

God continued to use the kindness of Christians to reach out to Nancy—to guide her into his preferred future for her life. She responded to an ad on a Christian radio station that urged abused women to call in. As a result, she enrolled in a class designed to help women understand what healthy relationships are like.

"During the class I was so shocked that I barely said a word. There were about ten women telling the same story as I was telling. Their ages, professions, denominational affiliations, incomes, education, and circumstances were completely different, but the stories they told were the same. They spoke of isolation; emotional, physical, and sexual abuse; intimidation; lack of financial resources; coercion; threats; and children used as pawns.

"Interestingly, *I was the only woman in my class who had actually left her husband.* The rest were hoping that they could learn enough about their contribution so *their husbands would change.* I could only wish them the best. I hoped and feared for them at the same time." Not long after, Nancy and her husband finalized their divorce.

During this time, the Holy Spirit began to draw Nancy toward her ultimate calling. She was hired as an administrative social worker by Northwest Family Life, a counseling center in Seattle.

While studying for a masters degree in counseling, she met Tom Murphy, the coach of her son's baseball team. She was attracted to him because of the way he treated all his players with respect. After dating for three years, they married. "But becoming a Murphy triggered an internal identity crisis," she said, and she met with her pastor about her guilt over remarrying. Finally, she recognized that she was no longer bound to the man who had repeatedly been unfaithful to her and so abusive to her and her children.

"During our first year of marriage, Tom told me that I had changed and he didn't like it. He asked why I insisted on consulting with him over every decision. I told him I was trying to be submissive. He told me again that he didn't like that. I asked him why, and he said, 'I miss you.' We'd been friends, equals as parents, and colaborers, and now he felt as if *I wanted him to be in charge.*

"I explained to Tom that within the conservative, patriarchal Christian traditions in which I'd been raised, submission was the norm and there were bad names for women who were seen as equals. Men were supposed to be the spiritual leaders. Exercising his newfound authority, Tom commanded me to live as his equal in our marriage. I laughed and obeyed. This dramatically altered the trajectory of my life and the example we set for our own children." Nancy continued her studies, earning a doctor of ministry degree while focusing on the theological issues that seemingly support violence and abuse.

Over the years she has become an international expert on domestic violence, traveling to places like Vietnam, Cambodia, Turkey, Poland, and the United Nations, where she has consulted with religious leaders, foreign ambassadors, and government policy makers. Nancy works with people who come from a wide variety of spiritual perspectives. She is a renaissance woman and is comfortable with both the downtrodden and diplomats. She is in love with Jesus, tempered in her expectations of church, and comfortable with men and women who view Scripture differently than she does.

Today Dr. Nancy Murphy *leads* Northwest Family Life (www.northwestfamilylife.org), whose mission is assisting individuals and families in finding hope and healing when caught in the destructive cycles of domestic violence. Domestic violence is one of the leading causes of death and injury to women around the world. Between 960,000 and three million women are physically abused by their husband or boyfriend per year.[1] Worldwide, at least one in every three women has been beaten, coerced into sex, or otherwise abused during her lifetime.

Nancy (www.nancymurphyonline.com) is in demand worldwide as a speaker. She teaches as an adjunct professor at several seminaries and advocates for women who are marginalized, powerless, and in pain. When she isn't on the road, Tom and Nancy split their time between Seattle and a small village on the west coast of Vancouver Island called Esperanza, where she first discovered the power of the talking stick.

• • •

My Take

Nancy was nearly crushed by the response of the church leaders in whom she first confided about her husband's abuse. Yet after receiving support from other Christians, she was able to find a way out for herself and her children. Rather than condemning the church for ignoring her plight for so long, she wrote God's Reconciling Love: A Pastor's Handbook on Domestic Violence *to equip them to help other victims.*

Nancy's life disturbs me. Hearing about the women she's protecting or the perpetrators she is trying to help makes me feel spiritually uneasy. I'm not only unsure if I could do what she does, at times I'm not even sure how she can work with both victims and abusers. To top it off, she spends a significant amount of time with First Nations people on Vancouver Island in Canada. Many of these people suffer from alcoholism and systemic abuse.

Somehow Nancy finds solace and inspiration by spending time with the suffering. I love Nancy's heart for the downtrodden, but her life convicts me. I have the utmost respect and admiration for her leadership, but I have no intention of following in her footsteps. Frankly, I lack the fortitude, will, and deep compassion that she exhibits every day toward the people who are trying to escape what she escaped by God's grace.

Fast Facts

84 % say **My church's perspective on the role of women in ministry is almost identical (27 percent), very similar (34 percent), or somewhat similar (23 percent) to my own.**

Our Bloggers Said

In a world where "God says it, I believe it, that settles it," it's sin to object to the teachings that women can't lead. And in that world you grow as a Christian by submitting and accepting. A lot of the questions are asking, in effect, "Are you growing as a Christian?" and who wants to say no to that?

■ ■ ■

I am not actively involved in a church right now, and one of the criteria for my next faith community is the affirmation of women as leaders.

■ ■ ■

Many times through lack of qualification and education there are no women capable of leading. Church leadership is a tireless job, and many women are busy with careers, children, grandchildren, and parachurch organizations. So I would have to agree with the statistics of these 603 women. To dispute these statistics is to continue a nasty trend of not believing women, especially church women.

■ ■ ■

I did a small qualitative study of evangelical women for my doctoral dissertation in 2007 and found that indeed, they say these very positive things. . . . They dismissed and invalidated the meaning of any experiences that didn't fit the "right" picture of the church.

Resigned To
I've Never Really Thought about It

Lee isn't on a mission to get women to do what she does. She is a schoolteacher raising three sons with her husband, Cliff. She believes a Christian woman could be the president of the United States but never the pastor of her church. In fact, if that ever happened, she would think seriously about switching churches. But the truth is, she never really thinks about it that much.

Like Lee, Kathy has never given much thought to how much influence women have in her church. As her daughters were growing up, she was just pleased that they willingly went to church and even found some good role models there. Yet when the question is raised, Kathy begins to see that, in addition to all the good her daughters received from the family's church, they may have picked up some not-so-positive messages that have hampered their church involvement as young adults.

CHAPTER 6

SATISFIED WITH THE STATUS QUO

The Lee Merrill Story

I WISH EVERYONE HAD a passion for the blues.

I could spend the rest of my life playing the bass in a blues band, backing up some killer guitar player, laying down a groove so wide you could drive a truck through it. But the reality is that a lot of people don't like the blues. As hard as it is for me to admit, many people don't have the slightest inkling what this style of music is—or even any interest in finding out.

The same is true when it comes to encouraging women to use all their God-given influence within the local church. Not all women are concerned about how women are or aren't being treated by the church. They just don't care. It's a nonissue. They're happy with the ways things are and have never really thought much about it.

True, this population skews more conservative in their cultural and theological leanings, but even moderate and liberal-leaning women report similar feelings when asked about this issue. My wife, who is in all ways liberal (culturally, theologically, and politically), has never spent much time worrying about women's rights in the church. This may be colored by the fact that she has no aspirations to be public and is married to me, which basically provides her with carte blanche access to any screen or stage I happen to be appearing on.

Lee Merrill is more typical.

A transplanted Southerner, Lee now lives in the Phoenix area with her husband, Cliff, and their three sons. She is a junior high special education teacher with a gentle sense of humor. When I first asked her to spell her last name, she said, "Like Merrill Lynch—but without the money."

Lee, now in her early forties, was born and raised in Shreveport, Louisiana. Her mom and dad both worked, so a nanny often looked after her. When she was young, her family attended church, though after a while she was the only one in the family who was attending regularly. When she was thirteen, she gave her heart to Jesus and was baptized. From that time on it was Jesus, Bible, and church. "My dad liked to say that I traded in my saddle for a Bible," she recalls.

Once she got her driver's license, Lee was at church whenever the doors were open, and she admits that one reason she was there so often "may have just been that it was an escape from my situation at home.

"My mom was very domineering and my dad was a 'yes,

dear' kind of guy—he didn't want to fight, so he would go out and push dirt around with his backhoe. I felt like my mom was being the boss and my dad wasn't stepping up to lead," Lee says. Her parents divorced when she was in college.

Lee got her undergraduate degree in elementary education. She then completed her master's in special education and recently earned postgraduate certification as a school guidance counselor.

Unlike his wife, Cliff grew up in a home with parents who remained involved in church—though a different kind of church. "Cliff grew up in a charismatic church with a woman pastor. She scared Cliff. He actually had bad dreams about her. Eventually his family decided to move to another church in their town. "I've never met the woman, so I can't judge her but . . ." Lee's voice trailed off since she was about to do something Christians try not to do—pass judgment on another believer.

Cliff works for Intel, which is how he and Lee ended up in Phoenix. He also serves as the volunteer worship leader at the evangelical church where they are members.

Since many of the women I interviewed for this book spoke with a fair amount of heat about the topic of women and the church, I was curious how Lee would respond to my questions. I asked her to describe the role women played in her church experience.

"Growing up in Shreveport, I didn't see women preach, but they could give a testimony in a mixed class [adult men and women]."

I asked her when women had to stop teaching boys; in other words, at what age did boys technically become "men," thus disqualifying women from teaching them any longer.

"It didn't really work that way, Jim," Lee said. "We had high school youth groups with women leaders coleading with the guys, but when the groups split up, they had guys with guys and girls with girls. I think it's more a relational thing than a biblical thing, though. I just have never thought that much about it."

I asked Lee if she would be *allowed* to teach the Bible on a Sunday morning to a mixed group.

"No, but women can share testimonies, Jim. For example, I sing in church a fair amount, and in between songs I *share* what the Lord has been showing me and how the song ties in with that. Also, we have a recovery ministry in our church for people dealing with addictions, and periodically a woman from that group will share a testimony about how God is working in her life."

Lee expressed zero angst about this arrangement and referred me to the most sacred text in Scripture for those who believe in the hierarchical God who is deeply committed to role distinction—1 Timothy 2:11-14. I asked her to read the passage to me.

A woman should learn in quietness and full submission. I do not permit a woman to teach or to have authority over a man; she must be silent. For Adam was formed

*first, then Eve. And Adam was not the one deceived; it
was the woman who was deceived and became a sinner.*

"So women are to remain silent?" I asked.

"Yeah, I know what you mean. When I read that today,
I thought to myself, *Okay, I'm not sure that I get the whole
silent thing,* but I did some studying because I was told you
might ask these kinds of questions. Here's what I learned. It
appears that the early church culture was very different from
ours. There wasn't a pastor or a music person or a church
staff. It seems like we would call their church services more
collaborative. So what I suspect is that the women must have
been interrupting the speaker or something. So Paul was telling them to talk things over with their husbands when they
got home.

"I mean, in the book of Joel, the Bible tells us that men
and women will prophesy, so women have to share what the
Lord is telling them—just not during the preaching, which
is what I think was going on here."

Some believers, I know, will find Lee's argument uncon-
vincing because she is essentially saying Paul was making
a cultural application. Others will discount it because her
exegesis is incomplete, but the fact remains that Lee came to
this conclusion after much reflection, prayer, and discussion.
"I talked this over with my husband," she said, "and all I can
say is I felt a peace in my heart about my beliefs on this issue."

After discussing this topic with people at polar opposite
ends of the issue, I've observed that Lee's approach to biblical

interpretation is common. When push comes to shove, *human beings do what they feel, not what they think.* This is how Lee and almost everyone else I spoke with navigated issues they didn't know how to explain rationally.

Nevertheless, I wasn't going to let Lee off the hook just yet. I asked her about the passage in 1 Corinthians 11:3-6:

> *Now I want you to realize that the head of every man is Christ, and the head of the woman is man, and the head of Christ is God. Every man who prays or prophesies with his head covered dishonors his head. And every woman who prays or prophesies with her head uncovered dishonors her head—it is just as though her head were shaved. If a woman does not cover her head, she should have her hair cut off; and if it is a disgrace for a woman to have her hair cut or shaved off, she should cover her head.*

"Lee," I asked, "in your opinion, why don't women—especially conservative Christian women—obey this passage? Why obey the one about being silent in church and not the one about wearing a head covering? I mean it's right there in black and white. Help me understand how you choose which one to obey and which one to ignore."

"Jim, that passage seems clearly a cultural issue to me."

And with that Lee was satisfied, but I wasn't. I tried one more angle in my search to understand how Lee was able to pick and choose passages from the Bible and not feel any anxiety about it. (To be fair: I do the same thing—cherry-pick—as do all Christians. We just usually don't admit it.)

I told her about something I had just read that day. "Lee, I was at the bank today and saw one of those trivia signs they put up to help dull the pain of standing in line—kind of like a fortune cookie for banking. Anyway, it said, 'The average woman consumes six pounds of lipstick in her lifetime.' Now I know that a lot of those lipstick-eating women are Bible-believing, on-fire-for-Jesus, stand-by-your-man Christians. My question is this: How do they biblically justify spending God's money on lipstick, given that 1 Peter 3:3 clearly says, 'Your beauty should not come from outward adornment, such as braided hair and the wearing of gold jewelry and fine clothes'?"

I reminded her that Christian groups like the Amish follow this to the letter, and even Muslim women seem more committed to these instructions than Christians. In fact, they view women who wear makeup but not head coverings as infidels. And given what the Bible seems to clearly say, they're on the solid biblical ground. I don't understand how churches pick one passage and completely ignore the others.

"Is this what you're doing?" I asked. "Picking and choosing?"

"No, Jim," she said, "I believe God created women to be a companion/helpmate for men. Unfortunately, the imbalance started in the Garden of Eden, when Eve went her own way and Adam just followed along."

Shifting the focus slightly, I asked an even more sensitive question.

"Lee, do you ever wonder if your parents' failed marriage informs how deeply you feel about this issue?"

Lee responded with grace and transparency.

"Yes, like I mentioned earlier, my parents' relationship was something of a power struggle, and that probably does influence me today. In fact, Cliff and I were discussing this issue recently, and he told me how important it was to him that I speak respectfully to him, especially in front of the kids. Men are made to lead and need our respect."

I asked Lee to play the Sisters Solidarity Sunday game with me.

"What would happen if all women and girls didn't show up at your church next Sunday?" I asked.

"It would be a mess, Jim, because the women in our church have great influence."

"So what wouldn't be happening?"

She quickly rattled off a list of positions and items that would be missing:

- A number of greeters
- The keyboard player
- The background singers
- Attendance would be down by 60 percent (meaning a total of 125 people would show up for the two services)
- Sunday school (*all* the Sunday school teachers for children and preschool are women)
- Bulletins

- Child care
- Adult classes for women

Lee couldn't imagine this actually happening. She was just being polite and playing along.

Again, not wanting to miss this rare opportunity to ask a conservative Christian woman her opinion about leadership, I asked Lee if she thought it would be okay for a Christian woman to serve as president of her husband's company, Intel.

"I wouldn't have any problem with that, Jim. Proverbs 31 talks about women being industrious, so I don't think that would violate Scripture," she said.

Unlike Leigh Gray, whom I interviewed earlier, when it came to national politics this Lee turned out to be more of a pragmatist. And while they both arrived at the same conclusion, they arrived there using different reasoning.

"So what you're saying, Lee, is that if a woman were running for the presidency of the United States, you would be open to voting for her, but if the same woman attended your church and wanted to be the pastor, you would vote against her?"

"Jim, in my mind spiritual authority is different from secular authority. To be completely honest, though, I prefer that a man be our president. However, if a man and woman were running and the male candidate wasn't an acceptable option, I would vote for the woman."

I asked Lee if the positions she said her church taught about women were in writing anywhere.

"You know . . . I've never really thought about it, Jim. I'll have to ask our pastor."

• • •

My Take

When someone I'm interviewing tells me, "I'll have to ask my pastor," I hear one of three things: (1) "Jim, I'm too polite to tell you what I'm really thinking"; (2) "Jim, you obviously haven't heard me and don't take my opinion seriously, so I will attempt to divert you by appealing to a higher authority"; (3) "Jim, I don't know the answer because what interests you has never interested me enough to inquire."

I could be wrong, but I suspect Lee fell into that third category. She didn't know if her church's position pertaining to what women are and aren't allowed to do was clearly stated on their website because she didn't need to know. Someone once said, "People see what they need to see." If that's true, then some readers will think that Lee is blind while others will think, This woman's got twenty-twenty spiritual vision. We see what we need to see and ignore what we don't need to see. Humans do this in order to filter out information we deem unnecessary or irrelevant.

Lee never called me back to tell me what her pastor said about their website, and I never checked it myself.

CHAPTER 7

I WONDER WHAT WOULD HAVE HAPPENED . . .

The Kathy MacKintosh Story

"You want green tea, Jim?"

I was running late for our appointment when my sister-in-law Kathy intercepted me via cell phone. She was already in line at Starbucks and, in typical Kathy fashion, had thought of me.

"Sure, Kath, I'll be there in five minutes. Thanks."

When I mentioned to Kathy that I wanted to interview her, Kathy was surprised. "I'm not sure why you want to talk with me, Jim. I haven't done anything unusual, and when it comes to your issue about women and influence in the church, I'd never even thought about it until you brought it up," she said.

Like her sister—who happens to be my wife, Barbara—Kathy is thoughtful and considerate. Yet when it comes to the paths they took after college, they couldn't be more dissimilar. Before we were married, my wife had gone right from college to the convent. Kathy took a more traditional path. She attended the University of Washington, where she met her husband, Pete. They raised four beautiful daughters. For the last twenty-five years, they've lived in a comfortable neighborhood on the east side of Seattle. They've attended a well-known, influential evangelical church for the past seventeen years and have remained faithful members of the same small group for over thirteen years. Pete and Kathy are *very* stable. They stick with their commitments.

I finally got to Starbucks, where my steaming-hot Zen Green Tea was waiting on the table. I gave Kathy a hug, and we got down to business.

"Jim, explain to me again what your book is about."

"Kathy, I'm trying to understand how women feel about not being allowed to have as much influence in church as they're capable of." She looked at me quizzically—an expression I've seen on the faces of other women who've never thought about this issue until I've brought it up. By this point in my project, it had become apparent that not all women think the church is repressing them. Kathy was about to explain why.

I'd never asked her how she'd come to faith, so I opened up my laptop, took a sip of my green tea, and asked, "How did you get started in this whole Jesus thing?"

Without hesitation, she began to recount what we used to call a "testimony."

"One day a few years after Pete and I got married, I was visiting my mom and dad. I needed some advice. I was actually facing a crisis of sorts. Certainly not the worst kind, but nevertheless important to me at the time. I was trying to decide whether I should continue to work in my chosen field as a dental hygienist. For one reason or another my mom didn't understand how serious this was to me and essentially said, 'Get over it and get on with it.' I didn't find her response that satisfying. It just so happened that my older brother Rick was visiting at the same time. Rick had become a Christian a couple of years earlier and was kind of a Jesus freak.

"Anyway, unlike my mom, he ended up listening to my concerns and questions for over an hour. Being a serious follower of Jesus, Rick sensed the opportunity to turn my everyday concern into an invitation to ask for God's help. He asked me about my relationship with Jesus and prayed for me right then and there. I found Rick's casualness somewhat startling, but moving at the same time. That experience marked the beginning of my journey with Christ. I started attending churches that taught the Bible and began to grow in faith and knowledge from that time up to the present."

Unlike many modern-day evangelicals, Kathy and Pete have done relatively little church hopping. They've attended just three churches in their thirty-five years of married life, and only two since they became parents.

Even though Kathy came of age during the tumultuous

sixties, she is no raging feminist. In fact, she told me she prefers that men lead the church, though I suspected her reasons probably had little or nothing to do with 1 Timothy 2. "What's that about?" I queried.

"What's what about, Jim?"

"Your statement that you prefer that men lead the church—where does that come from?"

"I like having men in charge," Kathy said. "I like feeling protected, and frankly I'm more traditional in that I prefer to keep things the way they are." Kathy is a modern woman. Once her daughters were in school, she began working outside the home. Recently she began working with Pete in his office. Having been raised a traditional Catholic, she had no exposure to the biblical arguments evangelicals use about women deferring to men. The Catholic church is as thoroughly dogmatic as any fundamentalist church about restricting ordination to men, pointing to the example of Jesus, who chose only males as his disciples, as well as the early church, which imitated Christ in restricting leadership positions to men. Many Catholic women, rejecting a teaching they find based almost entirely on tradition, gravitate toward a more progressive feminism.[1] Not Kathy. She found a profound sense of security and certainty in her new association with evangelical Christianity—particularly when Pete followed her lead and came to Christ too.

Wanting to reassure me that she wasn't a mindless stand-by-your-man kind of woman, Kathy offered more. "I'm not against women sharing in church; I'm just more comfortable with men having the last say. And one more thing—I believe more men will show up if men are leading."

With that my ears perked up. I'd heard this "more men will come if men are leading" argument in other interviews. It's a fascinating, and on the surface completely reasonable argument. If men lead, men will show up. If women lead, men won't show up. But wait—churches *are* led by men and yet *women* make up the majority of virtually every church in America. Ask yourself what would happen if women were afforded the same visibility and influence men currently enjoy. I wonder if it's the answer to that question that scares people away from giving women even more influence.

I felt as if I was finally beginning to get beneath the surface and into the truly personal issues that shaped my sister-in-law's views about women and church. As I took another sip of Zen, I decided to follow this trail. "Kathy, you just raised an intriguing topic I'd like to learn more about. How much would you say this issue about men coming to church because men are leading influences your views about the roles of women and men in church?"

"Seventy-five percent."

Kathy shot out her answer like an excited kid brimming with confidence, who raises her hand and jumps up and down because she *knows* the answer. With great confidence, zero hesitation, and no self-analysis, she repeated: "Seventy-five percent, Jim. That's how much this issue informs my opinion about the roles of men and women at church.

"I'd prefer a fifty-fifty split in terms of leadership from

the front," she continued, "but I'm a pragmatist, and I know that isn't going to happen."

I picked up some convoluted logic in her next sentence. "About 80 to 90 percent of the men in our church come because of the influence of their wives."

"So in a sense women are leading men, right, Kathy?"

"I guess so—kind of like the neck turning the head illustration. But once we get them there, we know they will stay only if they see men leading from the front, being in ultimate authority—in charge. If the roles were reversed, men would stay away. Now they come and later thank their wives for introducing them to the church and often to Christ. Men don't recognize their spiritual hunger the way women do."

"Kathy, are you saying that women are innately more spiritual than men?"

"Yes, in some ways, Jim. Women are more attuned to spiritual realities than men." Kathy paused a moment to take a sip of her drink. "Listen, don't get me wrong, women would love it if men could get there on their own, but for the most part that's not the kind of men we see around us. Women open men's eyes to things they wouldn't otherwise see."

"So, Kathy, you're saying it's not only acceptable but actually necessary for women to lead and influence men, so long as it's not done from the front. Am I hearing you correctly?"

She nodded.

Whether people realize it or not, who stands up front behind the pulpit raises the issue of symbolism. When the same person stands behind the same piece of sacred furniture week after week, month after month, and year after year, we subconsciously begin to assign special status to that person and that specific location in our sacred room. We assign a separate status to those who *don't* stand in that spot. The sheer absence of certain types and classes of people says something symbolically profound to us. While the actual words may never be uttered in public, the imagery does the preaching. Kathy had gotten the message loud and clear. Without anyone ever saying anything about it, she understood that men ran the church and women worked in it.

One of the questions I've asked a number of the women is, "How often have you seen a woman stand behind the pulpit and do exactly what your senior pastor does every Sunday?" In other words, how many times have they seen a woman teach the Bible with authority from the same location their pastor does in their church?

Kathy's response was not only quantitatively but also qualitatively representative.

"Three times, Jim!"

"You mean that in the span of seventeen years you have seen a woman teach only three times?"

"Yes, I knew you were going to ask me that, so I thought about it ahead of time."

Given the symbolic power of these three women, I was fascinated to hear more.

"The first woman," she said, "was a missionary talking about her work; the second was a recovery pastor talking about her program; and the third was a women's ministry leader promoting her work with women."

I told Kathy that purely in terms of symbolic value, none of them qualified as being on the same level of importance as her pastor. They weren't teaching the Bible; they were promoting a program or providing a sermon illustration for their pastor. The sheer infrequency of their appearances tells me everything I need to know about their perceived value in terms of influence.

Kathy's eyes glazed over just as I was finishing my philosophical rant. I'd lost her. She was staring over my shoulder.

"Hi, Barb!"

My wife had walked in behind me and was sitting a few tables away, not wanting to appear nosy. Kathy waved to her as I tossed her that "I'm busy" look spouses are uniquely trained to interpret and pulled Kathy back into the conversation.

"Have any of your daughters ever raised this issue with you, Kathy?"

"No, not that I can recall."

Finding this hard to believe, I dug deeper. "Even growing up in church, none of them ever asked you why women were not given access to the same levels of influence as men?"

Kathy is very sincere. She sat there trying hard to remember any occasion one of her daughters broached this topic.

"I'm sorry, Jim. I wish I could help you, but I just can't recall any situations where the girls asked me about this issue."

As I stared into the bottom of my venti mug pondering

my next question, Kathy interrupted my reflection. "Maybe it's because they had so many women leaders, Jim."

"Really? Who, when, where?"

"Most of the leaders they had from the time they were in Sunday school through their high school group were women. These women were especially influential in my daughters' lives during junior high and high school. But during the college years the ratio of women to men leaders changed, and I'm not sure why."

"So essentially your daughters did see a lot of women leading and influencing in the church they attended—the youth church," I said.

Kathy's eyes lit up. "I wonder why this pattern stopped during their college years."

I suggested that perhaps her church practices what Paul taught in 1 Timothy 2:12 concerning women not being allowed to have authority over men.

"No way, Jim," she said. "I don't believe that stuff, and I'm sure my church doesn't either."

Grabbing my laptop, I quickly typed her church's URL into the address bar. "Let's see if their policy about women leading is on their website." I entered the words *women* and *leading* into the church's search engine and up came . . . nothing. Or at least nothing that explicitly stated its formal position on whether women are *allowed* to teach men. This was not a surprise to me, since even the most conservative churches hesitate to put what they believe about this on their sites. In fact, that is why I've come to admire the fundamentalists who are proud to put it in writing—at least they're up-front about it.

"Kathy, maybe another way of asking my question is this: Why do you think women's influence in the church stops where the money starts?"

Seeing her quizzical look, I explained, "Having been a pastor for twenty-five years, I understand the inner workings of the church. I know where the money flows. It starts at the top and filters down. Because the evangelical church's most symbolically powerful location is the pulpit, and its most valuable asset from about 11 to 12 on Sunday mornings, one's income is largely determined by one's access to the pulpit."

I went on to explain that I believe men get preferential treatment over women in evangelical churches because (1) they believe more men will come if men hold positions of influence; (2) they believe women will follow (or lead) those men into this kind of church; (3) men are still seen as the head of the house and the high priest of the home. Churches want to reflect their support for that in their hiring policies and in the amount of money they pay men and women leaders on staff.

Now Kathy was the one staring into the bottom of her cup. She was lost in thought.

Sensing an important question, I waited.

"So I wonder what would have happened to my daughters if the church reflected what I really wanted?"

"What do you mean, Kath?"

"In my perfect church, Jim, there would be a fifty-fifty split between men and women leaders. I've always wanted more variety, including more men. I wonder why the church leadership never asks the people in church what we would like to see?"

"How does this translate into your daughters' spiritual development?" I asked.

"I just can't help but wonder if my girls would be in a stronger place spiritually if they'd seen more women leading and influencing. I wonder what would have happened if, as you say, women's influence didn't stop where the money starts. It really makes me think.

"Frankly, Jim, if I knew that seeing more women in leadership would have helped my daughters navigate early adulthood more effectively, I would say, 'Get more women in leadership roles.'"

After doing many interviews, I've come to understand that my sister-in-law's line of reasoning is reflective of many women who have been shaped by the nonfundamentalist but still fairly conservative brand of evangelical Christianity. Both groups look the same—women are largely absent from any roles associated with the highest degrees of symbolic power. What's fascinating and what Kathy's experience reflected was the very different ways by which the fundamentalists and conservative evangelicals have reached their positions.

Fundamentalists are proud biblical literalists. They take *the Word* seriously and do their best to ensure they're consistent with their positions. (Sure, they fail at times, but they tend to try harder than most of us.)

Conservative evangelicals like Kathy pick and choose biblical issues more judiciously. They're more sensitized to the culture and don't want to appear to be Bible-thumpers. But in the final analysis they often end up in the same place as their fundamentalist cousins.

Given the absence of a serious biblical rationale and her disappointment with some of the outcomes, I asked Kathy how she thinks she ended up believing men should have more influence in church.

In typical Kathy fashion with complete sincerity and transparency she said, "Two reasons, Jim. First, I've been conditioned to think this way. And second, I want men to feel welcome in church."

Her honesty left me with nothing to say. She was frank and forthright. She told it like it is. Because of the conspicuous absence of women in roles of symbolically powerful influence, Kathy had been conditioned to accept that men are uniquely gifted to lead in ways women aren't. This, coupled with her desire to see more men come to church, created a powerful subconscious acceptance of a situation she really didn't believe was best. The church leaders didn't need to say a thing. Their actions did the preaching for them. This approach essentially *dares* people to raise the issue—a spiritual version of "don't ask, don't tell."

I was curious as to whether Kathy would be interested in broaching this topic with people at her church.

"Kathy, how would you feel if I asked you to find out what your small group members think about this issue and then suggested you approach your pastor and ask him to provide you with a written explanation of your church's biblical rationale when it comes to denying women the same levels of influence they provide to men?"

After Kathy assured me that she would talk with her friends and pastors, we said our good-byes.

A few days later my über-responsible sister-in-law let me know what she'd learned. One of her church's women staff members sent an e-mail explaining to Kathy that women can be coministers with men on the staff and are given the title of "minister." (The title of "pastor" is reserved for men.) No woman could be senior pastor "because of the understanding of spiritual authority from Scripture." She assured Kathy that the elder board regularly reviewed this policy. Furthermore, she suggested the senior pastor could better explain the church's position on women in ministry.

● ● ●

My Take

I found it ironic that once again, a woman was told that the final word on how much influence she would be "allowed" to exercise would be decided by a man. But Kathy didn't give it a second thought, and she would not have given it a first thought except for her kindness to do this interview with me. I'm sure that her indifference will be bothersome to some of my liberal (or progressive, as they prefer to be called) friends.

But from my vantage point, Kathy most accurately represents the position of the average evangelical woman on this issue. Call it the result of conditioning, pragmatism, or (as some of my more conservative friends would say) a deep commitment to Scripture. In general, moderately conservative evangelical women aren't thinking much about this. They're often surprised to discover that their churches use the same scriptural justification for blocking women's influence as the more fundamentalist churches do. They didn't know because it didn't occur to them to ask. And their churches don't advertise their position.

Fast Facts

83 % say **My senior pastor is completely (42 percent), highly (26 percent), or somewhat supportive (15 percent) of women serving in leadership roles in our church.**

Our Bloggers Said

I've recently joined a big nondenominational church in our area. Women are elders on the board and in pastoral roles. However, the church also believes in marital submission, which I wholeheartedly agree with! I love my church, and I love going to church. . . . We must all do what God has called us to, but with the proper motives of serving Him through serving others with a spirit of love. . . . Personally, I find great satisfaction in cleaning my house and taking care of my children.

■ ■ ■

I was a pastor's wife for twenty-five years, and I can tell you that even if the pastor is supportive of women in leadership, that means very little if the denomination or board does not agree. When we voted in our congregation regarding women as elders—it was women who spoke out most loudly and passionately *against* it. Years of indoctrination by the church has led women to internalize these views.

■ ■ ■

I actually had the senior pastor in the fellowship I left just over a year ago say to me that the [*correct*] question wasn't . . . Can women lead or do women have equal ability to men? The [*correct*] question is . . . Does God allow it, and *the answer is a resounding no*. According to this pastor, God [*apparently*] gifts women in all kinds of leadership ways but then tells them to not use their gifts (unless they are under the authority of a man). No joke.

■ ■ ■

My two cents is that this is a good indicator of how deeply ingrained gender inequality really is in churches. And how most women just think "that's how it is supposed to be" because it's all they've been taught.

Resigned To
Making Trade-offs

Sandi and Amy are accomplished professionals. They excel at providing leadership to the men and women who report to them and work with them on the job site. But at church it's a different story. Both women actively serve in their churches but aren't asked or allowed to contribute as much as they'd like.

CHAPTER 8

HOLDING BACK TO AVOID PUSHBACK

The Sandi Horine Story

SOME PLACES WILL TAKE anyone—*even a woman.* Sandi Horine has poured much of her energy, passion, and skills into serving the church, both as a paid staff member and a volunteer leader, and she's learned this lesson the hard way.

Sandi spent her childhood in the mainline church, where her dad served as pastor. The official policy of that denomination eliminated the stained glass ceiling for women almost fifty years ago. Women are now permitted to lead at any level they feel called. So it wasn't until she began to run in more conservative evangelical circles that Sandi heard about the biblical restrictions pertaining to how much influence women were or weren't *allowed* to exercise.

Sandi is forty-six and is married to Mark, who until recently worked for a large insurance company in Cincinnati. They have two daughters and have lived in the same house for twenty years—pretty stable by today's standards.

Sandi and I met when we both worked on staff at a megachurch ensconced in the suburbs of northern Cincinnati. I was the leadership development guy, which meant I got to know the pastors, directors, and leaders of the various departments. Sandi worked in what some might call the social welfare department of the church. The needy who frequented Cincinnati's social service agencies showed up at Sandi's office as well. She was a case manager and program director.

When I visited her department, I couldn't help but notice that virtually all the staff members were women, even though more than half their clients were men. In addition to providing for the practical needs of her clients, Sandi also led a Bible study for them—something she wouldn't have been allowed to do with a group of middle-class men from the church. While that strikes me as a bit odd, Sandi was just happy to be able to follow her calling of serving the poor.

Sandi outlasted me as an employee at this church, but unfortunately after several years had a difficult parting of the ways with the pastors. She dropped out of church for a while but never dropped out of ministry. She just moved her love for the marginalized and the powerless to another organization, which was once again so desperate they were willing to take anyone—*including a woman.*

"I got a job teaching seniors at an inner-city high school.

My task is to get them ready for college. This school doesn't have that great a track record of graduating people from high school, let alone getting them into college, so my job can be intimidating to say the least. This is the most consuming job I've ever had. In fact, compared to this, my position at the megachurch was a walk in the park—but I wouldn't trade my current job for anything."

I asked her about safety. "I had a kid with a gun in my class," she told me matter-of-factly.

"Did you feel unsafe?" I asked.

"No, he had a drug deal to do after school and needed protection. He got caught and they slapped one of those electronic ankle cuffs on him and gave him probation. The cool part is that he's now in college, about to get a degree and a legitimate job. What makes these kinds of challenges worth it for me is that last year 71 percent of my students were accepted to college and were awarded over one million dollars in scholarships. This is definitely what I'm supposed to be doing."

Several years ago, Sandi's husband, Mark, lost his job and spent a couple of years unsuccessfully trying to get back into the corporate world. When a teaching position at Sandi's school opened up, he decided to apply.

"My principal was looking for someone to teach English. Mark applied and got the job. He also went back to school to get a master's in special education as an intervention specialist."

Their work life was looking up, but their church life

wasn't. However, with a daughter in high school, they were willing to try starting over again at church.

"A friend was planting a new church in another suburb, so Mark and I decided to give it a try. First, though, there was some unfinished business I needed to attend to. I had just read *The Shack*, a book in which the main character is asked to extend forgiveness to his daughter's killer. It was very moving.

"After reading that book, I realized I needed to extend forgiveness toward my former pastors. Even if they didn't respond in kind, I needed to offer it to them." Sandi and her current pastor met with her former pastor, who responded with genuine warmth, as she had hoped he would. "I could see the pain in his eyes," she says. "After we talked, we hugged, and it was a real hug, not just a polite hug."

I asked Sandi what had motivated her to go back to church. Did she feel guilty? Did she miss worship or preaching?

"The number one reason I decided to try again was because of my daughter. I felt I could trade a few years of my time to provide her with the opportunity to make a strong spiritual connection with God before she headed off for college. Along the way, I discovered that there were other things I really loved about the church.

"Our new church has about five hundred to six hundred in church each Sunday, and we have already been involved in another church plant. In fact, every two years our pastor brings on a new intern. After he has worked with them, they're sent out to start a new church in a place like the inner city of Detroit. We aren't into big buildings; we meet in a school.

"If it wasn't for this church," she concluded, "I wouldn't be in church. It is 80 percent great, and I live with the other 20 percent."

Because I co-own an Internet business called ChurchRater, I have a special interest in how people evaluate churches. I told Sandi, "Those aren't bad numbers. Let's start with the 80 percent. What gives them such a high ranking in your estimation?"

"Jim, the number one thing I look for in any church is a serious commitment to the marginalized and opportunities to serve the poor. In that category this church *gets it* big time. Even though we meet in a middle-class suburb of Cincinnati, poor people, and otherwise marginalized people, find their way to us and are warmly and genuinely welcomed.

"But it doesn't end with the church service. We also serve them where they live. In fact, I lead the ministry that reaches out to serve this population, and I feel very supported by the pastor and his staff."

People like Sandi make me feel lazy and selfish. What motivates someone who has a day job in the inner city to spend her weekends and some evenings doing more of the same? I would need a break, but not Sandi. She feels called to love these people, even if it means making some personal trades.

"Okay, how about the other 20 percent, Sandi? What's not working for you at your church?"

"Like I told you, Jim, I grew up in a denomination where women are at least officially allowed to have as much influence as any man. My new church, on the other hand, is male led with no women on the board of elders. Recently the pastor asked the church to put forward the names of some new elders, and during his talk said, 'Women cannot be elders because the Bible says that an elder is to be the husband of one wife [see 1 Timothy 3:2]. But what's confusing is that they do allow women to teach periodically on Sunday mornings."

"Teach the Bible to a mixed group?" I asked.

"Yes, Jim, and what I find duplicitous and even hurtful is that they *allow* a couple of women to teach even though the Bible explicitly says, 'I do not permit a woman to teach or to have authority over a man; she must be silent' (1 Timothy 2:12). On a personal basis, that's a nonissue since I have no desire to teach or to be a pastor. But what about the women who do? What are they going to think when they see that the Bible is being used quite literally on one hand to stop women from leading as elders and then interpreted not quite so literally when it comes to having women speak? It's like they're trying to have it both ways. So yes, I truly appreciate the fact that women are given the opportunity to speak, but what I don't like is the confusing methodology they employ when deciding which Scriptures are to be interpreted literally and which merely reflect cultural norms.

"An even more personally disturbing policy that my church's denomination has is that the pastors cannot meet alone with a woman unless there is a third party present. While I respect the intention of the rule, it makes meeting with the guy I work with challenging at times. He's suggested we meet at church during the worship service so we won't be alone. Frankly, this never comes up in business and I find it demeaning—like there is something innately tempting about me just because I'm a woman. On a practical level, it continues the cycle of male leadership since it's easier for them to get together with other men. Working with a woman adds an extra step."

Sandi was obviously frustrated and confused by the treatment she receives just because she is a woman.

"It's like gender trumps ideas, Jim. I asked my pastor once why the church doesn't include more women in leadership, and he said, 'There are no women stepping up.' I asked, 'So where's the pathway to step up?' The most visible women leaders oversee women and children's ministries. That really limits the number of roles for women or girls to aspire to. I actually think of my pastor as being quite progressive, but he says we will never have a woman senior pastor."

Sensing how deeply disappointed she must feel, I asked Sandi why she doesn't challenge the status quo and, if necessary, leave the church.

"I'm so frustrated about it I just block it out," she said. "It bugs me that there are no women in the decision-making group. I believe we need women—women are made in God's image too—*so leaving women out leaves God out*, but if I pick that fight then there won't even be women speaking. The

THE RESIGNATION OF EVE

few times I've tried talking about women in the church, they call me a women's libber or a whiner. The reality is that most women in the church accept this situation as normal—even some who hold high-power executive positions at work."

As I considered the implications of what she was telling me, Sandi spoke up. "Like I said, Jim, that's just the 20 percent. For now I choose to focus on the 80 percent that enables my church to be passionately committed to God's heart for the poor and the personal benefit my daughter, husband, and I get from the church. I feel very supported in what I love to do—not hindered at all—and my husband is thriving like never before. He agrees with me that the lack of women in leadership is not ideal, but he prefers that I don't rock the boat. I tend to agree with his approach, since on balance the benefits outweigh the costs to me.

"My daughter has done so well spiritually as a result of her involvement with our church that I would never do anything to jeopardize that. She lives in community with other college students, and they spend a lot of time praying and serving others. Yes, it does bother me that my daughter doesn't see women leading in our church, but the fact remains that if I went through everything I went through so she could end up here, it has been worth it."

Sandi is *resigned to* the situation. She's made a trade. Women do this all the time for their husbands, for their children, and for the opportunity to do *something* they love to do. The only difference between Sandi and a lot of other women is that *she knows she's making the trade* and has chosen to live with the tension. She's willing to exchange her comfort for the sake of others—her husband, her daughter, and even the poor and marginalized people she's come to love.

Having paid a high price for speaking up in the past, Sandi has learned to be more measured, selective, and cautious about what issues she chooses to take on.

"When I first got to our church, I expressed myself more often," she admits. "But like the proverbial jumping grasshopper in a jar that keeps hitting its head on the sealed lid, I recognize that it is fruitless to jump up and down, so I no longer bother with that. Now I find fulfillment at work—I use my leadership skills there and I take my brains there. *I've learned to hold back because I don't want to be pushed back.* It's all about making trades."

• • •

My Take

Forgive this gross generalization, but I've observed that when conflict arises, men often leave while women usually stay. Men don't like to feel loss. Men don't like to eat humble pie, negotiate trades, or admit error. This might just be my bias, but it seems to me that women are much more adept at the relational arts than we men are.

In any event, that would help explain Sandi's decision to remain in a situation she doesn't completely believe in. Undoubtedly, some will call her codependent, and others will call her a sellout, but for Sandi, "it is what it is." Bottom line, she puts her husband's and children's spiritual welfare above her personal fulfillment. While this choice may not satisfy those of a more liberal persuasion, Sandi (who is quite liberal herself) is willing to trade being misunderstood for her family's spiritual welfare and even her own happiness. Sandi knows that this season will pass, and other opportunities will come her way. She's willing to wait.

CHAPTER 9

YOU DON'T ALWAYS GET WHAT YOU WANT

The Amy Snow Story

WHEN I STARTED THIS PROJECT, I had no idea how I would find the "right" people.

I'm a big believer in following the leading of the Holy Spirit, which Jesus suggested is more art than science. To illustrate this, he used the metaphor of the wind. In John 3:8, he told Nicodemus, "The wind blows wherever it pleases. You hear its sound, but you cannot tell where it comes from or where it is going." Just as sailors need to be skilled at hoisting their sails to catch the wind, so we followers of Christ need to listen for the Spirit by putting up our sails and seeing what fills them. Putting up sails for this project meant sending a lot of e-mails, texts, Facebook messages, and phone calls to other "spiritual sailors" asking them to keep their eyes and ears open for the wind's movement. That's how I met Amy Snow.

I can't recall who introduced Amy to me. I happened to be traveling through her city when someone arranged for me to meet her for coffee. I had another meeting just before I met Amy in the same restaurant, and as I was ending my previous appointment, I noticed a woman sitting alone at another table. I asked if she was Amy, and she said yes. I meet quite a few people like this—anonymous "leads" who often become long-term friends. First impressions go a long way. I was immediately impressed with Amy; it was clear by the look in her eyes and the way she shook hands that she was a thinking, no-nonsense kind of person.

Amy is thirty-nine and has three children. Her husband pastors a mainline church, and she works as a chaplain in a downtown hospital. She not only cares for patients, parents, and staff, she also participates in research programs. Like her husband, Amy earned a master of divinity degree from Princeton Theological Seminary. However, she has no interest in being the pastor of a church, although based on my forty years of working with church planters and leaders, I'd say she clearly has the chops to do it. What she does want is to see women be given the same shot at leading as men. Her denomination "officially" has no stained glass ceiling, but as always it's the unofficial policy that determines what really happens on the street and inside the church.

I asked Amy to compare and contrast what her

denomination says in writing about ordaining and placing women in pastorates with what it does in practice.

"On paper, women are *allowed* to do anything they're called to do, including becoming the senior minister of a church.[1] In practice, most of them end up in one of two places—the university [such as Princeton Theological Seminary] or in a small rural church. In fact, I can't think of one 'big steeple' church [the mainline version of a mega-church] that has a woman senior minister."

Amy is a big thinker. Her eyes are intense. She fires off her opinions without fear. She expects to be taken seriously. Her chaplaincy gives her numerous opportunities to minister to people and to be intellectually stimulated. She currently participates in a research project on the religious coping strategies of parents whose infants and children have just been diagnosed with cystic fibrosis, as well as another on those of adults diagnosed with cystic fibrosis. She is also participating in a project to streamline the education process for those training to be hospital chaplains. She loves her work.

Unfortunately, the same can't be said of her relationship with her church. She told me about a disappointing interaction she had with a young boy on one of the rare Sundays when she preached in her home church. It turned out to be a tipping point for her.

"In our church, it's customary for the minister to stand at the door after the service and greet people as they leave. Since I rarely got this opportunity, I looked forward to it. As

I exchanged pleasantries with our parishioners, out of the corner of my eye I noticed a new family talking with each other across the room. They sent their young son over to greet me, so I was excited.

"Then he extended his hand and said, 'Great service, even if a woman isn't supposed to preach.' I was taken aback and told him that if his parents had something to say to me, they should say it themselves. I was appalled, but I knew he spoke words some people still feel, even in our church. This experience cemented my commitment to help create a church I would be proud to have my daughter be part of."

"But Amy, you don't even want to be a pastor in a congregation," I said. "Why the passion around seeing women achieve equal status to men in your church? What's your mission?"

After taking a sip of her iced tea, Amy said, "First of all, it's demeaning to women to tell them they don't qualify for a job simply because they lack a certain body part. Reverse roles for a minute, Jim, and ask yourself how it would feel if women were in charge and men were disqualified simply because they were unable to give birth. This is one reason women like myself migrate toward opportunities to minister outside the church where, frankly, it's illegal to treat women that way. More important, as followers of Jesus, when we block, stall, or divert women from using their God-given gifts—including leading—we are being unbiblical."

Unbiblical? I pointed out to Amy that I hear that same argument from people who hold the opposite view.

"Jim, the Bible clearly says, 'He called *their* name Adam,'[2] meaning God made man *and* woman in his image. We're a unit. We go together. If men dominate the story, we get a skewed picture of who God is, which may help explain the rampant spread of patriarchalism in the church. To be biblically faithful, we need women as well as men leading and influencing. That is the only way my sons and my daughter will get a complete picture of the God I love and want them to serve."

Wanting to lighten up the conversation, I decided to play Sisters Solidarity Sunday with Amy. I asked her what her church would look like if all the women in her church decided to take one Sunday off en masse.

She looked a little like Atlas deep in thought as she slid her hand under her chin and considered that scenario. Then she began to reel off a picture of what her church would look like without women. In addition to attendance being down by at least 60 percent, she said the church would have to do without:

- a director of Christian education
- custodial staff
- printed programs
- an organ player
- Sunday school
- child care
- the kids (except the few boys the dads might bring)
- most of the choir

"Who would be there?" I asked.

- the senior pastor
- the associate pastor
- the choir director
- the men of the choir
- the musicians in the band

Next I asked Amy to imagine how the church would change if women were free to lead, influence, and take any action the Lord led them to take in the church. What would that look like? What new things would we see?

"Well, Jim," she said, "that is quite a stretch, but since this is only a game, I'll play along." Then she began listing what she would like to see:

- A female lead pastor (along with a male lead pastor) in every church.
- The female pastor would be available to provide pastoral care and talk with women about topics like day care, breast-feeding guilt, sexuality, and periods.
- The men would teach at least half the Sunday school classes for kids.
- When women went on retreats, men would take care of the kids so their wives would feel supported.

Amy is a passionate follower of Jesus who wants to see these changes implemented, but she is also a realist, a mom, and a supportive wife of a man who is the senior minister of a growing mainline church in the conservative Midwest. She has chosen to make some trade-offs. She finds fulfillment outside the bounds of the church where she is free to operate and lead without restrictions. She is also on a mission to make changes in her little corner of the Kingdom.

"I don't want to overcorrect and alienate people we have relationship with, but I won't allow my daughter to grow up in an environment that demeans her or keeps her from becoming anything God has designed her to be. The trades are worth it for now.

"I do my best to teach my children my biblically based understanding of gender equality, and they see it played out in our home between their parents. I frequently correct their children's Bibles and Bible stories, substituting gender-inclusive language when appropriate. When my husband and I talk about God, we tell our kids that he is both 'a boy and a girl.'

"One Sunday I was sitting in the pew watching my husband give the children's sermon. I can't remember how it came about, but when a child mentioned God in exclusively male terms, my daughter—then five years old—turned and said loudly, 'God is both a boy *and* a girl. God is *perfect!*'

"Jim, to answer your question about my strategy for making changes, this is how I will make changes in my church—by teaching children, by modeling equality with my husband, by preaching and teaching God's Word with integrity when I am invited to do so, and by speaking out against injustice when the Spirit prompts me."

All Amy wants to see is women doing in the church what she lives out at home and on the job every day.

• • •

My Take

Amy was perhaps the most pragmatic woman I interviewed. On the one hand, she is very independent. Her day job is demanding, challenging, and stimulating. On the other hand, she is married to the pastor of a moderately conservative church and part of a denomination that, while openly stating women can be ordained, is having a hard time putting feet on that position. What's a smart, capable, and theologically savvy woman like Amy to do?

The aging process makes one acutely aware that life is about making trades. There is no green grass on the other side — the grass on the other side is the same color as the grass I'm already standing on; it's brown. Wherever I go, there I am. Like Amy, I've concluded that I don't get to have it all. While my idealistic self laments this, my pragmatic self points out that the clock is ticking. Amy has accepted her situation while simultaneously agitating against it. She hopes to make changes, but like most of us does not want to alienate people unnecessarily along the way. Until the situation is different, she'll apply the best parts of her creative thinking and leadership skills at her workplace.

Fast Facts

62% say *All* leadership roles are open to women in my church.

Our Bloggers Said

There are definitely places for a woman in ministry and it rarely includes leading a mixed [both men and women] Sunday school class.

■ ■ ■

Having grown up attending a Bible church in the Bible Belt, memorizing Scripture, attending Bible college, and teaching women's Bible studies for twenty-five years, I know that the reported statistics do not reflect the way many women feel. I have not been able to use my gifts to build up the church body. Males have always been in charge of decisions, with token females rubber-stamping their decisions. It is not safe to disagree, to ask questions, to go against the status quo. In our local church, women . . . don't seem to notice they have no say in things that truly matter. At 60 years of age, I have left the building with great regret and longing to be connected to a body of fellow believers.

■ ■ ■

Maybe the 62 percent who say that *all* leadership roles are open to them in their church mean that all leadership roles *they* think are appropriate for women are open to them?

■ ■ ■

At one church membership class I attended, I asked the pastor what the church's policy was concerning women— note: *there was no need to ask this question* about men, minorities, or any other people group—he stated to a room full of middle-class educated people that women were free to do anything at this church. They could preach, pray, prophesy, teach from the pulpit, do everything "except be a pastor or an elder, for we follow the Bible around here." But other than that, women could do anything. The entire room took his words in stride. Including me. Though I did not agree with him, I felt that unity was more important and that my view about women was simply a theological view.

Resigned From
Leaving the Church

The next stories introduce you to women who have considered walking away or who have already left churches, Christianity, and/or God. These women are not your go-to-church-on-Sunday-and-be-done-with-it types. They are leaders, influencers, and serious students of the Bible who, after taking a close look at their faith for a long time, became disenchanted, disheartened, or even indifferent toward church.

According to The Barna Group, more and more Christians are feeling their independence and beginning to explore new vistas. They're leaving churches they were once deeply loyal to and checking out other ways of practicing spirituality. Interestingly, women are at the forefront of this exodus. Laura and Kathleen are examples of this trend.

CHAPTER 10

EATING INTO THE PRINCIPAL

The Laura O'Neill Story

IF CHRISTIANS REPRESENTED different kinds of investments in the church's portfolio, Laura O'Neill would be considered part of the *principal*—the money you don't want to touch; the money you use to *make more* money (or, in this case, to make more disciples).

At fifty-three, Laura is in her prime of ministry effectiveness and isn't supposed to be losing interest in church—but she is.

She was raised in a conservative evangelical church but no longer considers herself a part of it. "I appreciate my heritage, but the fact is I'm no longer certain that I want to be identified with that denomination's politics."

Laura got started early with Jesus. "I don't remember *not knowing* who Jesus was or why he came."

She was eleven when God called her to the mission field. If evangelicals could be born Christians (they can't—they can only be born again), then Laura would qualify as their poster child. She has never wavered or wandered. To Laura, being a churchgoing Christian is like what being Catholic is to the pope. It's more than her faith; it's her people, her culture, her mission.

"I wasn't that impressed with celebrities and movie stars," she told me as we talked via Skype, "but missionaries, they were big time—I loved seeing how God touched the world through them."

Many years would pass, though, before Laura moved onto the mission field full time. After earning degrees in engineering and radiological science, she married Tom, the son of a missions pastor to Hispanics within the United States. Together they have served various churches throughout their marriage and raised two sons. Meanwhile Laura built a career in medical physics and Tom worked in banking and transportation.

Even as they were raising kids and building their careers, however, both felt drawn to serve in a Spanish-speaking culture. Several years ago, the couple connected with a ministry serving Mexico and Latin America and began working in Nuevo León, Mexico.

To help prepare Laura for our Skype call, I sent her some background on the "three resignations" continuum I introduced in chapter 1.

After we discussed her background at the beginning

of our call, I asked Laura where she'd place herself on the resignation continuum. "I see myself in all three," she told me. "I spent the majority of my Christian life in category 1 (resigned to) and am trying to get to category 3 (re-signed). Currently, though, I find myself teetering on the knife-edge between categories 2 (resigned from) and 3."

Laura's version of resigning from church is much more subtle than people who leave without letting the door hit them in the backside. As I would come to learn through other interviews, Laura's experience is quite representative since women *often leave the relationship before they leave the room.* Their hearts precede their feet. Sometimes they don't even know that they're getting ready to leave. They're experiencing what I call resignation creep.

"I seem to be distancing myself from religious obligation," she said. "For instance, Tom and I just recently returned to the States for a furlough from the mission field and have temporarily moved to a new city. Normally one of the first things we do when we're in a new place is to find a church home—it's what you do. But right now I find that I'm not all that highly motivated to find a church. Maybe it's that resignation creep you mentioned, Jim."

Laura is a no-nonsense woman—the kind of person you'd want to lead any kind of project launch. Her day job as a medical physicist is demanding and requires high-level decision-making skills—something she feels uniquely qualified to exercise.

"According to the DISC test [a well-known leadership

style test], I come out a high D (dominating). That's considered an asset for a man, but when one of my pastors saw my results he said, 'That's really tough for a woman'!"

"Was he saying that to comfort or warn you?" I asked, with a not-too-well-hidden dash of cynicism.

"No, Jim, he was just trying to tell me that it would be a challenge—that I wouldn't be well received. He didn't tell me what to do about it," Laura said.

Laura was staring at the ceiling trying to find the right words to describe the angst she's learned to live with simply for being born the "wrong" gender.

"I've wondered so many times why God would give me this personality with characteristics that would only frustrate me my whole life. I don't mind at all doing domestic stuff, but it can't be the sum total of my existence for long. I don't mind doing the behind-the-scenes serving stuff; in fact, I rather enjoy it," she said. "But that's not all of who I am. I don't crave public recognition, but some of what's in me simply requires visibility and access."

Tom and Laura once began attending a church that described itself as purpose driven. Its vision statement included a commitment to "reach beyond." Given her missions experience and leadership gifts, Laura thought she'd found an ideal opportunity to use her influence. Before long, though, Laura realized the church would never act on any of her suggestions. "I found myself trying to lead from the backseat," she said, "and I don't do that very well."

Having spent time living overseas and being something

of a wannabe missionary myself, I asked Laura about how her experiences as a woman leader when she was in Mexico differed from when she was home in the States.

"Tom and I have been ministering in Mexico for the past three years. Between the two of us, I'm a bit more proficient in Spanish, so I do get more opportunities to speak. But even though one of the Mexican pastors invites me to preach, I'm not sure he's really listening—"

I interrupted her. "Are you saying that you preach in Spanish without using a translator?"

"Yes," Laura said. "It took a while, and there are still some topics where I lack vocabulary, but for the most part I can hold my own in Mexico. But to answer your original question, unlike in the States, where I'm essentially forbidden to speak from behind the pulpit to a mixed audience, in Mexico I get a hearing. Like I said, though, I'm still not sure I am heard."

"You mean you get the stage, but you don't get the credit?" I asked.

"Something like that, Jim. It's kind of hard to explain, but in essence what I feel has happened is that the evangelical West has successfully exported their theological paradigm—including the limitations on women—to the developing south, resulting in a very mixed message for this *machismo* culture. They need us to train and teach, but they don't want us to get too much exposure, which is another reason I'm losing interest in going back."

Listening to Laura lose heart for something she's spent

years developing a passion and unique skill set for reminded me of a sermon author Calvin Miller gave to the Baptist Women's Missionary Union several years ago:

> Women are more likely to go to the mission fields
> to be a doctor or a nurse or a teacher, I think,
> than men are. Once they get there they can work
> with a situation by living in it better than men
> can. They can more easily embrace people of
> other faiths with other value systems than men
> can. In short, they are able to go more slowly in
> redeeming a complicated world than men are,
> and in going more slowly they change the world
> about them, step by credible, slow-paced, and
> very human step.[1]

Like Laura, I have a deep love for and interest in other cultures, so it was sad for me to see someone as capable, curious, and willing as her having second thoughts about returning to work among the people she loves. So often it seems *it's not the work but the workers* who discourage us from wanting to try again. Another loss for the Kingdom.

Because we were on video Skype, I could see Laura stare-searching for a way to explain all of this without sounding like she was picking on any denomination in particular and evangelicals in general. She kept making passing references to "culture," but I sensed from the look in her eyes she meant it in a negative way.

Wanting to shift the topic and keep the conversational momentum going, I decided to jump into the "culture wars" conversation. Having been born and bred in a conservative denomination, Laura, I was certain, would be well versed in its political and cultural rhetoric.

"So, Laura, when I hear you say 'culture' I feel like I'm hearing you say 'liberal feminist movement.'"

"Jim, if you look at history—anytime women take over, the men just quit. They stop, they sit down, and they don't do it anymore. We've emasculated our men. We've become too aggressive."

"What about you, Laura? You're a medical physicist. Do you earn more money than your husband?"

"Jim, I'm speaking out of both sides of my mouth because I'm conflicted about wanting to have more freedom but worried about how men will interpret it."

"So is it your job to care for men's feelings, Laura?" I asked. "That's how it sounds to me. You make them sound like the victim."

Out of a desire to change the subject, avoid conflict, or broaden the conversation, Laura said, "Women are good ones to represent those who 'don't have permission.'"

Permission! That word kept surfacing in many of my interviews. I asked Laura, "Why is it that women need 'permission'—they need to be 'allowed,' but men don't? I don't get it."

Laura stared at the ceiling. "I guess men do sometimes, like when young men need to be given permission to preach."

I explained to her that what she was describing was a normal developmental process—one that could apply to either men or women.

I was pressing this issue with Laura for three reasons: first, she cares; second, she's thoughtful; and third, because "all transformation is linguistic"[2]—that is, words frame ideas in the same way a picture frame focuses our attention on an image.

As we struggled to understand the meaning of each other's words, Laura replaced the phrase "*given permission* to preach" to "*being invited* to preach," a subtle but telling change.

I asked her about this—I wondered if she knew she was doing it.

"You've hit on a very sensitive topic," she replied. "How does a woman lead a man without chopping his legs out from under him, or on the other hand, becoming an expert at playing the power of suggestion game?"

What Laura was articulating was the skill of indirect influence many women have acquired in order to be taken seriously in a man's world. She had learned that what she couldn't say directly she could suggest as a possible idea that the pastor could then adopt as his own.

My guess as to the real reason Laura was reluctant to use the word *permission* is that she was trying to avoid sounding like a feminist. She didn't want to make men look bad. The somewhat innocuous replacement phrase "not invited" sounds softer and is easier to digest, making those in power appear more thoughtful and even kindhearted.

This subtle change in language—from permission to invitation—makes it appear as if men haven't really given that much thought to the issue of women and influence. In fact, nothing could be further from the truth—just consider the plethora of books written by and primarily for pastors on this controversial topic.[3]

The fascinating thing about all this is that the rules outlining acceptable roles for women within the church are largely unspoken and often unwritten. In researching for this book, our organization contacted the church Sarah Palin attends in Wasilla, Alaska, to see if they had anything in writing that clearly states what they practice regarding women and preaching—namely, that while Sarah Palin could be president of the United States, she will never be "invited to" preach the Word of God in that church. They had nothing available in writing that clearly states this, though as you'll discover in chapter 19, the church's senior pastor clearly states this position in a sermon available by podcast.

Could it be that male leaders intuitively recognize just how bad this would look in writing and consequently avoid putting it in print?

While this may seem a prudent way to keep the peace, the net result is that they will continue to lose some of their very best influencers and leaders, like Laura, to churches and secular organizations who don't require a gender test.

• • •

My Take

One of the most alarming trends taking place in the church today is that long-term insiders like Laura and Tom are looking at options other than conventional church to satisfy their spiritual hunger. By the time leaders like these two veteran missionaries begin asking why the church is so slow on the uptake regarding women, you can be sure that multiple thousands of the less committed have already left the building.

What's interesting is that many of these church dropouts are not Kingdom dropouts. Like Laura and Tom, these "revolutionaries," as George Barna calls them, often invent new ways to express themselves spiritually, even self-funding their spiritual enterprises while keeping their day jobs. When the church loses leaders like Laura, that's what I call eating into the principal.

CHAPTER 11

SHE LEFT THE HOMESCHOOL CHURCH

The Kathleen Felmey Story

KATHLEEN FELMEY WAS one of fifteen women I met with over two days in Portland, Oregon. My friend, blogger and author Pam Hogeweide, had arranged for the women to meet with me to tell me their stories of faith—and sometimes of frustration.

Kathleen was the most serious Christian I met over those two days. She was the only one who brought along her Bible, as well as other literature she wanted me to read. She was prepared for battle, a soldier for Jesus with fire in her eyes. Kathleen was fearless and above all *earnest*—and I'm a sucker for earnest.

I came to faith in the late sixties during the Jesus people

era. I didn't join a church for two years because I was too busy trying to "save" people. Thanks to Hal Lindsay we were convinced that Jesus would be coming back no later than 1975. When you're convinced that Gog and Magog are going to descend from the North (a.k.a. Russia) and invade Israel, your view of reality becomes skewed and your sense of time speeds up. Suddenly you begin to "see" evidence of your beliefs (the European Common Market) and ignore anything that runs counter to it (the information age).

In any event, Kathleen's fervor reminded me of my own as a young Christian, so I asked her to tell me her testimony (something we did for entertainment back in the day). Kathleen told me she had not been raised in a Christian home. "Mom was a bartender and Dad was a retired Coast Guardsman, but mostly he was an alcoholic. The only literature my parents read were magazines. The Bible remained on our bookshelf, untouched. I did have a children's Bible with an absurdly golden-haired Jesus on the cover. It also had pictures of the devil that made me afraid. I wondered if Satan was really that ugly.

"When I was seven years old, I found out from a friend that Jesus lived in the clouds. Once that revelation got through to my little heart, I began swinging on my swing and singing 'Jesus Christ, Superstar' to the sky above, hoping he was listening.

"In my early teens, I was diagnosed with insulin-dependent diabetes," she added. "It completely changed my life. I battled teenage depression, poor health, and suicidal tendencies."

After Kathleen graduated from high school, she moved out into her own apartment. She met her husband while living there. They moved in together, and for reasons she can no longer recall, they started attending a little country church that had been started by some on-fire Jesus people.

"These silver-haired, spiritually seasoned brethren welcomed my boyfriend and me into their world, which is where I was introduced to Jesus and the Bible. Instead of bars, we went to Bible studies every Friday night." Soon Kathleen and her husband became engaged, and shortly after the birth of their first son they married, in 1986. She was twenty years old.

"Given our shaky beginnings, it will come as no shock to you that we struggled in our marriage. Money was tight and my already-not-so-great health took another hit following the birth of two more children."

Because Kathleen is diabetic, her pregnancies were high risk; however, her fourth pregnancy brought even more challenges. In fact, her fourth child, Jennifer, was born with a congenital heart defect. "After loving and caring for her through several surgeries," Kathleen said, "she passed away in her sleep in 1997. She was just two and a half years old. We were devastated. Sadness settled over our lives, and we sold our home to get away from the pain."

Eventually the family found a new home east of Portland. As life began to feel normal again, they discovered a church that included a number of families who, like the Felmeys, homeschooled their children.

My conversation with Kathleen about her spiritual

pilgrimage was triggering all kinds of memories for me. In 1977 after seven years of "training" in an independent Pentecostal Church in Seattle, Barb, our three kids, and I moved about ninety minutes north to "plant" our first church. We met in the rented hall of a Christian school. We welcomed the lonely, broken, and desperate for friends—people just like Kathleen and her boyfriend (now husband)—and led many of them to Christ one by one.

We also homeschooled our kids for a while. My wife had her teaching credentials but didn't like teaching. In addition, the state of Washington didn't sanction this form of education back then. Nevertheless we forged ahead. I found it appealing largely because I love anything subversive—especially when it's done in the name of God.

Unfortunately my wife's dislike for teaching didn't abate, so she would organize the kids' education around various TV shows. Their favorite class, which was designed to teach them maritime skills, was called *The Love Boat*. Eventually we sent our kids to a private Christian school where someone else taught them to read. (Not to worry—they've all been through college and two of them have graduate degrees.) Kathleen's homeschool experience, however, wouldn't have the same happy ending.

"We had been looking for a church that welcomed homeschooling families—a community that shared our beliefs." At first they were convinced they'd found the ideal church for them. Although they enjoyed worshiping with fellow homeschoolers, however, Kathleen began to feel uneasy as she realized that joining this church also meant adhering to a number of spoken and unspoken rules, particularly about keeping women "in their place" at home and church.

"They taught that limiting the size of your family through birth control demonstrated a clear lack of faith in God and disobedience to his Word," she said. When Kathleen asked what couples who were infertile—whether unintentionally or not—were supposed to do, she was told they should adopt. If, however, a husband had had a vasectomy, or a wife a tubal ligation, reversal surgery was encouraged and viewed as an act of repentance.

In what Kathleen began to call "the Proverbs 31 trap," she sensed that her womanhood was being contrasted with that of the elders' wives. She was encouraged to reserve her best efforts for cooking, teaching her children, choosing her wardrobe, and buying the best natural foods. These, she felt, were viewed as a test of how committed she was to God.

"The rule I found particularly demeaning to women was the 'microphone rule.' Our church prided itself on being open to the leading of the Holy Spirit, meaning people in the congregation could prophesy so long as it was done 'decently and in order.'"

Kathleen then pulled out the visitors' handbook from the church and showed me the section that outlined the rules for this part of worship. It began by acknowledging that the Holy Spirit might prompt believers to use their spiritual gifts to build up the others present. It then explained that all men,

ages thirteen and above, were free to speak. Women, however, were required to ask their husbands for their oversight
before they could speak out loud. They explained this by
quoting the apostle Paul: "The head of every man is Christ,
and the head of the woman is man" (1 Corinthians 11:3).

"So a thirteen-year-old boy could speak into the microphone without checking in with anyone," she said, "but if I
wanted to do the same thing, I was required to get my husband's permission. The only reason for this difference was
my gender."

Although that bothered her, it wasn't enough to convince her to leave the church. Women like Kathleen often
will absorb insults aimed at them, but if you try it on their
kids or husband—watch out. She noticed her pastor beginning to emphasize the importance of training one's children
to be entrepreneurs, and then he warned of the dangers of
letting teenagers work in fast-food restaurants.

"Since my husband manages a fast-food restaurant, you
can imagine how insulting this was to my family," Kathleen
says. "My husband blew it off, but I was done. He stayed,
but I decided to take a break from church.

"Jim, during this break I had numerous encounters with
God. He began to open his Word to me. All of a sudden,
I could see his love and his truth about who I was to him.
I discovered that he died to set me free, not only from sin
and death, but also from the expectations put on men and
women. I worshiped him. Tears of joy flowed freely. This was
the kind of love I'd been looking for all my life. Something

shifted in me. I began to see the Scriptures in living color; they were alive to me."

Kathleen loves the Bible. She told me that on several occasions in the days when she attended this church, she sat around a table discussing Scripture with some of the elders. She was often the only woman at the table; the others had gotten up to do the dishes. For a moment the elders would seem to forget that she was a woman and would interact with her as an intellectual and spiritual equal. But at some point they always seemed to remember that they weren't supposed to engage in such discourse with a woman and shifted the conversation to more mundane topics.

"After a couple of years away, I decided to give the home-school church one more try," Kathleen says. "But one Sunday they began to teach from organizations that promote biblical patriarchy and complementarianism. I knew I didn't want to expose my daughter to this. We walked out in the middle of that service, never to return. This time my husband joined me."

At about this time, Kathleen, who has always enjoyed writing, began to blog. "I finally had an outlet for my brain, and I couldn't believe the freedom." At first Kathleen says she wrote mostly about the pain and sadness caused by the teachings of her former church. "I soon discovered that I wasn't alone," she added. "Many other women online were journaling their experiences as well."

In the church, Kathleen had been told to run theological questions past her husband, "the spiritual leader and resident theologian of her home." So perhaps she shouldn't have been surprised when her former pastor decided to confront her indirectly after reading her blog.

This pastor called her husband, suggesting that he direct Kathleen to take down a blog entry where she had criticized the pastor's extrabiblical teachings. "By this time," Kathleen said, "I'd tasted freedom, so when my husband approached me, I informed him that there was no way I was going to take down my blog! If our pastor had approached me directly, I would have *loved* to discuss why I didn't agree with his teachings, but that call never came."

There was no glee in Kathleen's voice when she discussed this incident. "I was sad about the way the whole relationship unraveled. There were many things about that church that I loved and many people there whom I admired."

● ● ●

My Take

Unlike some who stop going to church altogether, Kathleen is no quitter. "My family and I are currently waiting for God to show us how and where to find fellowship with a community of believers. It's our desire to find people who are willing to dialogue, listen to each other, and learn to love each other in the same way Jesus loves us."

She's even been able to see a silver lining in all the difficulty. "This journey has actually put us in contact with many nonbelievers whom we've been able to minister to. We show them a 'nonreligious' way of walking with and loving God. I am blessed!"

For now, she says she is simply on a long hiatus, waiting to find the right kind of church. While some may find this disturbing, at least Kathleen wants to go back. Even though she hasn't yet found a church, Kathleen is one earnest follower of Jesus, and she hasn't stopped reaching out to people through her blog and in person.

It's hard to believe, but our culture is currently witnessing the end of a five-thousand-year era. In the past 150 years the world has witnessed dramatic, startling, and rapid shifts in technology, industry, military might, communications, and human awareness, but the "strongman at the top" leadership model has continued to prevail . . . until now. We are finally witnessing the end of "might makes right," and Kathleen is one of the foot soldiers in this battle. Kathleen and millions of others (mostly women) are proving that when people have access to information (Google and Wikipedia) and the ability to share that information (Facebook and Twitter), they reverse that old saying "right makes might." Those who resist this trend will be on the losing side of the battle. Better to join them and even invite them to say what they're really thinking.

Kathleen is a homeschool mom, not a radical feminist. She loves the Bible and really wants to raise her kids in church. Instead of putting a bit in her mouth, leaders would be better served by giving her a microphone. Instead of stifling the conversation, they should ask her to lead a discussion about how to make the church a place where women can flourish. As Clay Shirky says, "The future belongs to those who take the present for granted."[1]

Fast Facts

81% say **I strongly (55 percent) or somewhat (26 percent) agree that my church provides women with the same degree of leadership opportunities that Jesus would give them.**

Our Bloggers Said

I think women (and many men) leaving the church to function in their calling is . . . truly grievous. What is left in the church is a form of religion without all the gifts present and working. I think what people miss in the Gospels is that Jesus wasn't into religion either. He was the one going around talking to women and touching lepers—which were huge religious faux pas. . . . Francis Schaeffer points out that by calling Mary to his feet in the Mary/Martha scenario, Jesus is calling her to become a disciple. Traditionally, she wasn't even supposed to be in the room and Martha was being the righteous one. But to be called to come and learn from *the* teacher was truly radical!

■ ■ ■

Most of the comments [seem to be] made by people who, consciously or unconsciously, think of "leadership" in terms of power and prestige, rather than service. Perhaps the women approached in the survey understand what Jesus meant when he said: "Whoever would be great among you must be your servant, and whoever would be first among you must be the slave of all. For [even] the Son of Man came not to be served but to serve" (Mark 10:43-45, ESV).

■ ■ ■

To bash all the males is really unfair. Females who want to be in leadership need to look at their own motives. Everyone needs to ramp down their aggression and hostility concerning gender issues in America. Jesus taught cooperation among males and females, not competition.

■ ■ ■

Though I am one who has "left" the big church, I am no less involved in the growth and health of the body of Christ I call home. Additionally, oh do I understand the bossy women dynamic. They go to house churches, too, and cause a lot of trouble there as well. I also understand the need for doctrinal understanding and training. Without sound teaching we are vulnerable to feminism. Without sound teaching I have also seen a pendulum swing the other way. There seems to be "new" teachings out there that come just short of women donning head coverings. Paul warned us long ago about the doctrines that would skew the true revelation of Jesus. We are no less vulnerable today.

■ ■ ■

I would have to respond in the "Amen" category with the women in this survey. Women in church are much happier women. Especially if they stick to the teachings in the Bible, which show that Jesus is 100 percent in favor of cooperative leadership rather than some male to female gender quota. . . . Creeping American women's liberation theology has made it very difficult in the church in terms of male to female ratios in leadership.

Resigned From
Leaving the Faith

People (even Christian people) wonder how a loving God could allow billions of humans to live and die in squalor. They also wonder why this God doesn't intervene and stop the handful of jerks who mess things up for the rest of us. Helen Mildenhall is very bright. She was once a deeply committed Christian, but after years trying to make sense out of church these kinds of questions overwhelmed her sense of reality and she walked away from God.

Susan found something in therapy that her theological studies failed to explore: human beings don't live in categories or compartments. Upon discovering this truth, she began the long process of applying it to her young life. This journey eventually led her to become completely disinterested in church and Christianity. "Whatever" expresses how she feels about it all today.

CHAPTER 12

WHOSE JESUS SHOULD I FOLLOW?

The Helen Mildenhall Story

HELEN AND I FIRST MET ONLINE. By the time we got to our first meeting over coffee, each of us knew a great deal about how the other thought and felt about important topics. That's because we had first connected by dialoguing at one of Off The Map's websites. I had hired an atheist to attend church and write reviews, which we then posted at the *eBay Atheist*. Helen regularly commented on the posts.

Because of her intelligence and wisdom—not to mention her technical know-how—Helen quickly emerged as the unofficial moderator of the blog. I was the official moderator, but her humor and tact made it a much stronger site.

Helen's story is compelling. It's filled with twists and

turns in which she came to faith, only to lose it. Here's why she resigned from believing in God.

Helen was born and raised in England. One of her great loves has always been music. From an early age, she excelled at classical violin and piano and has been involved in community and church orchestras.

"My parents weren't religious, so I wasn't exposed to evangelical Christianity until I was in college. I embraced it enthusiastically. When I prayed and gave my life to Jesus, I felt a strong and powerful presence. That convinced me Jesus was real and had answered my prayer. It was one of the most exciting things that had ever happened to me."

Helen began praying, reading the Bible, and attending services at a small charismatic fellowship regularly. "The members were excited to hear about my conversion, and I loved the joyful worship," she says. Some of her new friends recommended a tape series that explained basic evangelical theology to her.

"I was shocked when I put the introductory tape in and heard that the Bible is *the Word of God*. It wasn't just a reliable record of Jesus' life written by humans as I'd thought. I was to treat every word as if God himself wrote it!

"I was taken aback, but I decided to give this and the other teachings on the tapes the benefit of the doubt unless I had evidence they couldn't be true. Wasn't that what faith was about, after all?"

Helen sought "to be the best Christian I could be," but there was one problem. Her boyfriend, Steve, was not a

Christian. Despite her earnest prayers that he would embrace Christianity, he showed no interest. She couldn't understand why God wasn't answering her most important prayer request. At least not yet.

I asked her what her new friends thought about her relationship with Steve. She said they told her she "should end the relationship since the Bible says, 'Do not be yoked together with unbelievers'" (see 2 Corinthians 6:14).

Helen says, "It was easy for them to say. Of course I wanted to please God, but Steve meant a great deal to me too. I remember thinking, *Why didn't God save me before I was dating anyone? Then I wouldn't have gotten into this situation.*"

Helen tried to end the relationship the following summer but found it too difficult. Instead she and Steve became engaged and made plans to move to the United States after graduation. Steve was accepted into a doctoral program, and as a dual citizen of the United Kingdom and the United States (her mother is American), Helen had no problem moving to the Chicago area with him.

"I very much wanted to go, but I prayed and told God, *If I don't get any job offers I'll take that as a sign I shouldn't,*" she says. She received two job offers from actuarial consulting firms in Chicago.

Soon after the couple moved to the city, Helen went to a Christian bookstore and asked where she could find a good Bible-believing church. She was referred to a large evangelical church and began attending every week.

"Because I was engaged to Steve, I stayed on the fringes

of the church. I'd made up my mind to marry him and was tired of being advised not to." Knowing none of the pastors at her church would perform the ceremony, the couple asked a chaplain affiliated with the university Steve attended to do it. "He was happy to conduct the ceremony," Helen says, "and I was pleased to have a 'somewhat' Christian wedding."

As Helen happily settled into her new life with Steve, her work life was going well too. She passed her actuarial exams and was promoted quickly. That is when Helen noticed that women had the same opportunities as men at her office—but not at her church.

"My church had no women pastors or elders because they believed the Bible forbade it," she recalls. "For a while I wasn't sure what I thought about women church leaders, since I couldn't accept that women were less capable of leading than men in general."

I asked Helen whether she was afraid to disagree with her church's official stance on women.

"Actually it was about trust rather than fear. I was giving the Bible the benefit of the doubt, and I trusted that my church's restrictions on women along with all their policies were based on clear teachings in the Bible. I assumed that churches that had women leaders must be ignoring what the Bible said because I hadn't been exposed to their reasoning.

"At some point I ran across some writings based on the Bible that taught that God wanted female as well as male church leaders. I was pleased and privately adopted that view. It made much more sense to me than my church's belief, and

I preferred what it implied about God's view of women. It wasn't enough of a deal-breaker for me to change churches: since I didn't aspire to being a church leader it didn't personally affect me. I decided not to discuss my new views with my church leaders because I didn't think there was any possibility of them changing their beliefs."

Helen's comment reminded me that while many women hold views that differ from their pastors', they rarely express them and are almost never invited by anyone in authority to share them.

"Like most evangelical churches, my church believed the husband was the head of the household and the wife was to submit to him."

Guessing that as a non-Christian Steve wouldn't care about the "submission" issue, I asked Helen to explain.

"Steve didn't care what evangelicals believed about husbands' and wives' roles since he wasn't a Christian. And he would never have considered using a belief that wasn't his to try to get his way at home—he was far too honest and respectful of me. That suited me, so in practice Steve and I were equal partners. Steve was fine with me being as involved in church as I liked as long as I didn't push him to have anything to do with it. I would have loved him to be interested, too, but I appreciated that he didn't try to discourage me from participating."

Helen decided she wanted to become an official member of her church, and the church permitted that as long as Steve had no objections (he didn't). After joining the church,

Helen became more involved in Bible studies and other activities. "I enjoyed the extra teaching and time with other Christians," she says. "Now that I was married they wouldn't advise me to divorce Steve, so I was no longer afraid to get to know other people at church."

Once Steve had finished his doctoral program, the couple had their first child. Helen was able to leave her job and stay home full time with their son.

"Evangelicals approve of mothers staying home with their children, which was what I wanted to do anyway," Helen recalls. "I was invited onto a church committee for the first time: the nursery committee!"

About two years after the birth of her son, she and Steve had a daughter. Just before their little girl's first birthday, however, Helen's world was turned upside down.

"Steve noticed I was increasingly saying weird things and behaving strangely. I had no idea. I was involved in doing a number of things I believed God wanted me to do, and I was quite happy. In fact, I had just convinced a prominent apologist to post the transcript of his debate with an atheist online after finding only the atheist's half of the debate posted.

"I asked the apologist to release his transcripts even though the atheist who'd made the debate transcripts told me it would make no difference. I appealed to Genesis 50:20, 'You intended to harm me, but God intended it for good' to suggest that no matter what the atheists intended, God could do good with his words. I was delighted to get a letter back from this Christian scholar a few weeks later saying he'd changed his mind because of what I had written. He allowed his transcripts to be posted on a Christian site and be seamlessly linked to the atheist debate page." Helen was excited by her success and convinced she had personally heard from God about writing to the apologist in the first place.

Helen's behavior and words became more bizarre, so early one morning Steve called her mother for advice. When he told her what was happening, she realized Helen was probably having a manic episode. She was familiar with the symptoms because she had seen them often in a manic-depressive family member.

Helen's mother told Steve to take Helen to the emergency room. "After finding someone to watch our kids, he drove me there," Helen said. "A typical symptom of mania is thinking nothing is wrong, though my thinking was quite delusional. I took a Bible with me to the ER because I believed God had chosen me to 'find the mistakes in the Bible.' Believing God has chosen you for a special task is another classic symptom of mania."

Helen's animated speech, emotional volatility, and rambling answers made it obvious she required treatment, and she was admitted to the psych unit.

After she grabbed another patient to get her attention, Helen was locked in the "quiet room," a room with no furniture, except for a mattress on the floor. A camera on the wall enabled the staff to monitor what she was doing.

Things went downhill from there. Her husband was sent

home, and three nurses ordered her to take some pills—or else they'd have to inject the medication.

"I was very upset," Helen says. "As confused as I was, I had read my patient rights sheet they gave me at admission and knew I had the right to refuse medication.

"Once alone again, I could tell things weren't going well for me. I decided I'd made a mistake by straying from my beliefs. I reaffirmed my belief in Jesus as Lord and walked around the quiet room singing a simple worship song. I started feeling better and I felt that Jesus was telling me— through an inner thought, not an audible voice—that I should trust and cooperate and then everything would work out okay.

"The kindest looking of the three nurses came into the room with some food. He said he liked my singing. I ate the food, lay down, and went to sleep. The next morning I woke up back in my regular psych unit room."

That same day, her doctor told her that she had bipolar disorder (formerly known as manic depression).

"It was difficult and humbling to hear that I had a serious mental illness," she says. "That's how everyone would view me from then on. My life would never be the same."

Since Helen was cooperating and had "good family support," she was discharged and sent home with instructions to see the psychiatrist the hospital staff recommended. A few weeks later, Helen happened to meet a psychiatrist at church. "That seemed like a 'sign,'" she recalls. "I very much wanted a Christian psychiatrist who would respect my beliefs."

About six months after beginning medication and out-patient treatment, Helen's condition had stabilized. She had been put on leave from the nursery committee at church; otherwise, she experienced no problems there. Her psychiatrist eventually let her stop taking medication. Helen resolved to follow a healthy lifestyle, hoping to prevent a recurrence—even though she knew the illness almost always reappears without medication.

While researching bipolar disorder online, Helen began participating in online discussion forums. She quickly discovered the help such mental health support forums provide. Before long, one site owner invited her to be a moderator, giving her access to edit or delete posts when necessary.

"It didn't seem appropriate talking about what Jesus meant to me on the mental health forums," Helen says, "so I set up my own website where I could do that and linked to it from my forum posts."[1]

The fall after her daughter turned two, Helen got involved in an intensive Bible study program. Unlike other women's Bible studies she had attended, this class was highly structured with weekly lectures, study notes, and questions. Helen loved that the group leader kept the discussion focused on the week's material.

"I remember walking into the sanctuary just as the meeting was beginning that first week and being surrounded by the sound of women singing hymns. I felt at home," she says. "This was a *serious* Bible study—just what I was looking for!"

By the end of the year, Helen had become the group's

regular piano player, accompanying the women as they sang the opening hymns. "One of the side benefits was the teaching leader's weekly call to me telling me which hymns to prepare," says Helen. "During the call she'd often share thoughts about the upcoming lecture she was in the middle of writing. I enjoyed those phone calls, and they helped us get to know each other."

The next fall, Helen became a group discussion leader. She worked hard to be prepared for every session and especially enjoyed the opportunity to "shepherd" other women through regular phone calls with each one of them.

At about that time, she and Steve moved out of the city. Helen began attending another church closer to her home. She quickly felt comfortable there. Not only did her new church hold the same basic beliefs as her old one, they invited her to serve on the website committee. When a discussion board was added, she became one of its moderators. She also played regularly in the church's orchestra.

Helen began attending a Bible-based weight-loss video workshop that her church hosted. Its basic teaching was simple: don't eat until you feel hunger and stop when you're satisfied. Rely on God to help you not to eat when you're not hungry.

Helen was pleased as she began losing some weight, but something about the course's theology bothered her. Not long after, the organization's founder was embroiled in a controversy over her views on Jesus and the Trinity. Helen was the first in her church to be aware of it, and after she presented her findings to the church, it stopped hosting the workshop.

"I felt it was my duty to warn other Christians about this group, too, and devoted a lot of time and energy to it," says Helen. She contacted many other churches that were holding the workshops, and eventually she was mentioned in stories by the *Wall Street Journal* and *Christianity Today* that covered the controversy.

Helen then confronted some of the leadership at her Bible study about the group's articles of faith and even individuals' leadership styles. "I didn't realize it at the time, but my behavior revealed an uncharacteristic lack of inhibition suggesting that I might be getting ill again." When the area leader asked to meet with her, Helen was told she needed to stick to her discussion leader responsibilities only.

Helen recalls, "She didn't understand why I would even think I should be critiquing the program's articles of faith or my leader. How could she? She'd never had that manic belief I had that God had called me to some particular assignment and I was to obey him, regardless of what other humans thought."

Helen had been open with others at her church about her bipolar diagnosis, and now people there were beginning to treat her differently as well. Some got angry and set limits to protect themselves from her. "The senior pastor asked me not to e-mail him anymore," she says. "When I asked if I could meet with him one-on-one, he said no. I was removed from the website committee and banned from posting comments on the discussion board. Things were going downhill."

Since my own extended family has been significantly impacted by mental illness, I felt bad, not only for Helen, but also for the people who didn't understand how to be helpful. She was confused that other believers were treating her like a disobedient Christian when she was only doing her best to obey what she believed God was telling her.

"It hurt when other Christians disapproved, but I couldn't let that dissuade me from following God. I didn't realize I was becoming ill and had the impaired judgment and lack of inhibition typical of mania."

Steve was also beginning to get concerned. Helen was acting more and more as she had when she was first diagnosed as manic. He urged her to go back to her psychiatrist, which she agreed to do.

Though Helen went back to her doctor because of the promise she'd made to Steve, she refused to go back on medication, though she did agree to return every few weeks so he could monitor her condition. Just after Thanksgiving, her illness escalated further. "My behavior in the Bible study leaders' meeting was noticeably bizarre, and a few people called Steve, concerned about me. Steve took the next day off work so he could drive me to the psychiatrist.

"On the way to the office my heart sank as I realized that I'd lost control. I wouldn't be able to refuse meds and drive home like I had previously. I was quite delusional. My husband took a route that I wasn't familiar with and it was snowing. I started to wonder if I had died and was in some strange afterlife state."

Because Helen seemed to be exhibiting symptoms of epilepsy as well as mental illness, her psychiatrist wanted the office neurologist to run an EEG trace. Confused and afraid of the procedure, Helen refused, despite repeated attempts by her husband and the doctors to convince her. Finally, they told her she would be hospitalized unless she agreed. She thought about how much she had hated the powerlessness of being in a psych unit during her first illness, so she reluctantly consented. After being started on medication again and having the EEG procedure, she was allowed to go home.

The next day, still quite ill, she stopped her "correct theology" campaign directed at the weight-loss program. She started wondering about her motives and worrying about what her actions might be doing to the group's founder, whose beliefs remained unchanged.

Helen says she looked at herself and didn't like what she saw. As a Christian, she believed in being kind to others. Her website, which she called "Love Is the Most Excellent Way" after 1 Corinthians 13, was supposed to embody that. Was being a member of the "doctrine police" and impressing other Christians with her theological expertise really what following Jesus was all about? *When had being right become more important than being kind?* Helen decided to apologize to the group's founder and was pleased to receive a kind note back in return.

Not everyone was so affirming. Even Helen knew she could no longer be a Bible study group leader, but she hoped she could still attend the group. Instead she was told she couldn't return to her class—or even a different class under the same area leadership.

"That was painful to hear," Helen says. "I wanted to get well again and knew it was important for me to be with supportive people who weren't freaked out by me. By distracting me from my internal delusions and by being role models of what 'normal' was, they helped me reconnect with reality. I found another Bible study that I could attend instead."

She also found herself under new restrictions at church. The associate pastor discouraged her from any one-on-one contact with the senior pastor and instructed her on how to give constructive criticism to church elders. She was not allowed to play with the orchestra or post on the church discussion boards she used to help moderate.

"All these restrictions were humiliating," says Helen, "but I stayed. It gave me an opportunity to be with friends and also the chance to earn people's trust again." She even found a group under a different area leader that accepted her—and it was less than a thirty-minute drive away.

I asked Helen if she was able to forgive those Christians who had reacted to her with such fear and coldness.

"I didn't want to be angry with the Christians whose treatment had hurt me. I knew Jesus had said unless I forgave others I wouldn't be forgiven. When I considered that those people were probably doing what they thought Jesus wanted them to do, it helped me forgive them. On the other hand, it didn't help my faith at all. I believed Jesus loved without limit and took risks with people, like when he touched the person ostracized for having a contagious incurable skin disease. My Jesus seemed to be different from theirs. (I liked my Jesus much better.)

"The problem was that we were all getting our understanding of Jesus from the same Bible. Since I'd come to believe in the Bible as God's Word, I'd assumed people who honestly studied it would come to the same conclusions I had. Why wasn't that happening?"

Helen says she discovered something else about the Bible when she was ill. "I managed to self-justify a lot of my illness-influenced behavior using Bible passages. It was easy to find places where God asked people to do something everyone else thought was crazy—like Abraham sacrificing Isaac.

"The different Jesuses people followed and the ease with which I was able to support my delusional thinking biblically shook my faith in the Bible. If what the Bible taught wasn't clear, how could I be sure anything evangelicals taught me was true? And what was the point in studying the Bible if I couldn't be certain of my conclusions?"

Helen realized that her faith in the Holy Spirit had also been affected. "I was disappointed that the Holy Spirit hadn't given other evangelical Christians the insight and ability to handle me differently. They hadn't been any kinder to me than people who weren't Christian. In fact, they'd often been meaner, since they viewed me as a disobedient Christian. People who weren't Christians were less judgmental of me because they didn't hold a moral yardstick against me."

Something fundamental had shifted: "I stopped giving the Bible and my evangelical beliefs the benefit of the doubt," says Helen. "I realized I might lose my belief in God altogether, and wondered how I'd survive emotionally if I did. Yet it had become stressful to pray to someone who might not exist. I also wanted to get away from delusional thinking, and prayer had been all mixed up with that. I wanted to limit my thinking as much as possible to concrete, externally testable thoughts like, *It's time to take my children to school because the clock says 7:45.* I decided to stop praying and see how that went."

The changes in Helen's faith and behavior were private and internal. She kept going to church and Bible classes and didn't talk about her doubts and prayerlessness. She gave the "right" answers to the questions but was not sure she believed them anymore.

"I was no longer afraid of losing my faith, but I was afraid of losing my friends," says Helen. "I might get ill if I withdrew myself from my social circles or introduced stress into my relationships with Christians by being honest." She felt better when she was invited to serve as the orchestra's librarian. She noticed that, when she was in the church office, the pastors seemed comfortable engaging in brief discussions with her again.

Still, she felt like a hypocrite as she realized her former beliefs were not coming back. "My illness didn't return, but neither did my faith. After four years and no symptoms I finally felt strong enough to handle the social ramifications of leaving church and Bible study." When she told her kids about her decision, she said she'd be happy to continue dropping them off for youth classes and activities. They told her they didn't care if they didn't go back either.

About six months after leaving church, Helen learned about an unusual eBay auction from two sources, the atheist discussion board and her former pastor's blog. Hemant Mehta, an atheist, was auctioning his soul. In other words, he would attend the church of choice of the highest bidder for a year.

"I felt sorry for Hemant," said Helen, "expecting a very zealous Christian who didn't understand atheists to jump at the opportunity to try to convert him." Curious to find out the outcome, she was surprised to discover that my organization, Off The Map, had "bought" Hemant's soul. Instead of having him attend one church for a whole year, we were sending him to a dozen different churches once. And instead of pushing him to be converted, we simply wanted his feedback on the church visits.

"I started reading Off The Map's *eBay Atheist* blog just as Hemant began posting his church reviews," added Helen. She appreciated the way Hemant and other atheist blog visitors were treated. "I'd never seen an evangelical pastor treat atheists with such respect."

That's when Helen and I began to dialogue online. She told me about her experiences as a Christian and the problems she had with Christianity. She told me she was pleasantly surprised that although I was a Christian, I didn't try to argue her back into her former beliefs. Conversing with me helped her feel less alone with all her questions about evangelical Christianity.

Once I got to know Helen, I asked her if she wanted to help manage Off The Map's online presence. She agreed, telling me she appreciated Off The Map's goal of "helping Christians be normal." Not only did she become our blog manager and webmaster, she volunteered at a number of Off The Map's conferences.

Helen sums up her attitude toward Christianity this way: "Although I would never put myself under the authority of a church leadership again, I appreciate much of what I learned in my years in church and from the Bible. I know many wonderful people who are Christians and like being friends with the ones who are happy to be friends with me.

"I still have a great deal in common with anyone who wants to make a positive difference in the lives of those around himself or herself. That's how it should be if the Bible is true, since it emphasizes 'love God' and 'love your neighbor' and indicates they are inextricably linked."

• • •

My Take

Helen changed my life. Much of what I've learned about dialogue came from observing her interactions with the people who hurt and disappointed her—Christians. Cyber communications can be brutal and mean-spirited. Having the freedom to say something without having to personally face—or even see—the one being critiqued can make for a very unbalanced communication process.

Watching Helen interact with Christians around hot topics with grace and kindness made me a better person. I learned the art of restraint from Helen. I learned the importance of not comparing my best with the other person's worst, and I learned not to run away when someone strongly disagreed with me. Many times on our website, frustrated and mean-spirited Christians would attack Helen. I would watch her work with them using Scripture and patience.

Helen can't quite bring herself to say she is an atheist, so I came up with "almost an atheist." Since Jesus told us to judge a tree by its fruit (not by its name), I can say that I see Jesus in Helen.

CHAPTER 13

CHANGE A METAPHOR, CHANGE A LIFE

The Susan Hall Story

THERAPY IS THE ART OF changing a person's controlling metaphor.

Is your glass half full or half empty?
Are you a spender or a saver?
What color *is* your parachute?
Are you a victim or a victor?
Are you mostly a "me" or mostly a "we"?

In one of my graduate classes, the professor said, "If you can change a person's metaphor, you can change his or her life." After about ten years of pondering his statement,

I finally "got" what he meant. This is the world therapists, counselors, and professional helpers live in—the world of the mind and imagination. Next to marketing professionals, they probably understand the human psyche better than anyone.

Susan Hall is a very successful therapist and entrepreneur. She's in her early forties, single, and no longer a believer. What's most disturbing about that is it probably didn't have to turn out this way. During her youth and early adulthood, Susan was the consummate Christian insider. When she was just eight years old, she felt God tell her that someday she would "lead all of Africa to Christ—the entire continent." She was born and bred in Indiana, home of the Gaithers and Sandi Patty. She was educated at one of the most conservative evangelical colleges in America. For the first twenty-five years of her life, she never wavered, skipped church, or wandered away.

How did she get from there to here?

How did the church lose such a precious investment?

What did therapy do for her that theology didn't?

How did she get so detached from church that the subject doesn't even make her mad anymore? She's just indifferent to us now.

I met Susan at her office, which is located on the top floor of a small but impressive five-story building situated just north of downtown Seattle, complete with a beautiful view of the nearby harbor. I asked her about her business because it was evident from her office and the professional way she presents herself that Susan is all about doing business.

"I've discovered that I like doing business deals as much as I like sitting with patients," says Susan. "It became apparent to me several years ago that most therapists do not know how to find good commercial space, and when they do, they are too risk averse to pull the trigger and actually lease the property. I like doing that, so I'll go in and rent a suite of offices and sublet the spaces. In fact, I just leased space for nine more offices, which will double my capacity at this particular location."

As you can see, Susan is a go-getter. She has three businesses: Susan Hall Properties, which leases properties and subleases office space; Seattle Therapy Alliance, which focuses on low-cost individual therapy for women; and Ra'ah Counseling and Seminars.

"Jim, many of my colleagues think they're selling themselves," she says. "I think I'm selling what the client wants, which is typically happiness, freedom, or relational connection. I work with my own clients to help them find the satisfaction they're looking for."

Susan didn't start out thinking she would become a therapist and entrepreneur. She originally planned to spend her life expanding the Kingdom of God and serving in the church.

"In my early adult years, I invested in the church because I felt that the institution was working toward *my* larger goal, which was serving God and bringing salvation to the world. I didn't have a sense of my own efficacy in that, but I did have a conviction that I could do my part within this larger vehicle."

During elementary school, Susan was the kind of Christian who made sure everyone could see the "Jesus is #1" sticker on her notebook. She had an insatiable spiritual appetite, was wild about God, and was quite certain that she would end up in full-time missions someday. Unlike many college students who begin experimenting with new ideas once they're away from the influence of home, Susan remained focused and on fire for Jesus.

She says, "My most serious act of rebellion was choosing a church in a different denomination. Growing up, my pastor was pretty much into hellfire and brimstone. I found switching to a church where I actually liked the pastor was quite freeing."

One year after college, Susan started a women's shelter for her church. She served in that capacity for six years. This is when she began reconsidering her faith.

"I found myself reflecting on the difference I was experiencing between the God the church talked about on Sunday and the God the women talked about during the week. While the Sunday conversation at church seemed most focused on following the rules, the weekday conversation with the women was more about knowing 'the truth about me,' or personal brokenness. At church I had to hide my thoughts, questions, and life choices. I began to realize that something was missing at my church that I could find only at the shelter." Confused, Susan began seeing a counselor to help her sort out this apparent discrepancy.

"My therapist, who was not a Christian," recalls Susan,

"would listen to my struggles around church and say, 'What you're telling me makes it sound like your church is unsafe,' to which I responded, 'They are unsafe. I can't tell them what I'm really thinking or doing, and that bothers me.'

"I worked long and hard in therapy in many ways, especially to grow a self I could love and respect. I eventually realized that I could either be about protecting a self-interested entity [the church] at my own expense, or I could get about living into my own passion and promise. I started to believe that I could do anything that I wanted to do, and it blew open my future."

Not long after this therapy session, Susan quit her job at the church and made one of the most impulsive decisions of her life. She decided to move to Seattle and enroll in graduate school.

"To this day, the decision to move to Seattle for graduate school remains one of the smartest things I've ever done. For the first time I was exposed to the idea that psychology and spirituality do not need to be walled off from each other. I discovered that God is not surprised or perplexed by the human experience." Eventually she earned a master's degree in counseling.

When Susan first moved to Seattle, she planned to join a church. "Being a good Christian," she says, "I church-shopped, looking for the right fit. After several failed attempts to find a church that was more interested in helping people navigate the complexities of life and less about maintaining the religious status quo, I finally admitted to myself that I was done with church. I quit going and haven't been back since. But I didn't quit my faith—not yet. I still considered myself a Christian, even if it was the non-churchgoing type."

While still a graduate student, Susan accepted a staff position at a Christian organization. With her nose for business and passion for expanding the Kingdom, she thought her gifts could benefit this fledgling organization. And while she excelled at setting up seminars and retreats at which the men she worked for could speak, she was not invited to use her own voice. "I ended up wearing several hats and eventually burned out. I realized that those who were supposed to be practicing mutual respect were in fact exploiting my goodwill and talent. This was my second experience with a Christian institution failing me."

While Susan is a tough, competent woman, she had been led to believe that if a woman wanted to go places, she needed to attach herself to an influential Christian man. So when she began dreaming about starting her own private therapy practice, she began questioning herself.

"Jim, I didn't think I could do anything by myself," she says, "because as a Christian woman, I'd learned that I needed a man to get places. But the reality is that I was seeing ten patients before I had even left my full-time job and hung out my own shingle. So I decided to take the knowledge I'd acquired setting up those retreats and seminars and use it to launch my own practice. Soon I was teaching seminars and accumulating more clients than I could personally handle. This is what led me to start Seattle Therapy Alliance."

Susan was done with church, with institutions, and with the idea that she needed men to open doors for her. But she still wasn't done with God—not yet.

"Spiritually those years were a wasteland for me, Jim. I wasn't going forward or backward. I wasn't sure what to do with this faith piece that had been such a big part of my life from the time I was a little girl. I grieved the fact that I no longer had a heartfelt relationship with God. I grieved that I didn't fit into a spiritual community of any kind because I've always had the safety net of a believing community around me. God and I seemed like two married people who had grown apart. We were living under the same roof but never talking, connecting, or being real with each other. It was during this time that I discovered feminism."

A few years ago, Susan wrote an article about the pathway that led her from evangelicalism to feminism. In it, she recalled how the churches she observed as a Midwestern farm girl allowed only men in the pulpits and in leadership. They did so based on their conviction that "men were created by God to lead, and women were by nature the midwives of life. . . . [so] it was only natural that women would be in the nursery and kitchen. . . . With this spiritual 'reality' so universally accepted, I was left to squelch and eventually submerge my burgeoning gifts, questions, and desires."

Susan resonated with the feminist literature she had begun reading. She began taking classes at a mainline seminary, where she worked toward her doctorate in international feminist theology. As she pursued her doctorate, she determined that the faith tradition in which she'd grown up expected its adherents to accommodate sexism "under the guise of woman's so-called need for protection."

> It was institutionalized Christianity's sneaky way
> of getting women to endorse the idea that their
> inherent inferiority and evil-doing made them ill-
> equipped to hold positions of power, while at the
> same time making women nearly solely responsible
> for raising up the next generation of leaders.
> I quickly understood why feminists called their
> interpretive method a "hermeneutic of suspicion."[1]

Susan realized how far apart she was from the faith of her youth during a class discussion one day. "The professor asked us what church meant to us. I responded that for me it meant being together with people who were being real and who were about the work of loving one another well. She said, 'Church is a gathering of believers in Christ.' At that moment I realized that I had to decide if that was what I believed. I felt I had had years of truly sacred 'church' experiences with my women's therapy group. Some of the members were not Christians, so I had come to believe that Christ was not central to the active creation of 'church.' I had to face the fact that I was no longer a Christian."

Her newfound conclusion was strengthened during her international challenges as part of her doctoral program. As she listened to feminist theologians from a wide variety of cultural viewpoints, she realized that she could no longer believe in a God who was a patriarch and that she couldn't support any patriarchal system. She decided she must be an agnostic.

Because several of my close friends and colleagues are atheists/agnostics and because being an atheist nowadays comes with almost no price tag, many people claim atheism as their nonreligion of choice. I asked Susan if she was an atheist or an agnostic.

"Depends on the day, Jim," she said. "One thing I know for sure, I'm not an anti-theist like Richard Dawkins. I still have clients who present spiritual issues to me in therapy, and I would never do anything to take away their faith or commitment to Christ. All of us need something to help us make sense of the world. I just find that I don't need a god (or God) to help me do that anymore. I'm good with people doing whatever they need to do. I just don't want them to impose it on me."

I was intrigued by Susan's nonchalant attitude about God. Many who have put in as much church time as she has end up bitter, angry, and reactive toward him.

"A big part of my indifference," she explains, "comes from having worked out my relational patterns with narcissistic, self-focused male leaders. I grew up in a milieu in which everyone orbited around a central figure and protected his interests at all costs, even to our own detriment. We all played supporting roles, and our own lives were simply not the point of our existence. Over time I looked at the church the way I look at a narcissistic family. So it was natural for me to shift that allegiance to the church when I moved out of my family home.

"I truly wanted to accomplish huge things for God, but in my early adult years I believed I could be successful only if I grabbed hold of the best coattails around me and rode them to a place of power and influence. I didn't want to be famous; *I just wanted to have the power to achieve change.* I didn't believe I could do it, though, as a young, slight-of-stature woman. I didn't have any sense of my own capability and efficacy.

"Therapy helped me discover how to stop doing things that were detrimental to me in order to make someone else happy, which is what I had to do with the church as well. I had to detach and focus on living my own life and passions. Now I can do my work, and it doesn't have to be attached to an institution, particularly a patriarchal one."

Having convinced Susan that her only value was in "accomplishing big things for God," the church failed to develop her and eventually lost her.

She found a better metaphor for her life in therapy than in theology.

She found a system that allows her to bring all of herself into her life experience.

She found a way of life that she says fills her with joy, wisdom, and love.

Now she doesn't even miss the church—she's just indifferent to it.

• • •

My Take

Susan's story may be difficult for you to digest. It's hard to listen to indifference, particularly when it's coming from a former insider. Susan was a passionate follower of Jesus. She idealized the church and its leaders. She was ready to sacrifice, work, and do whatever it took to see the Kingdom of God come to earth. In that respect she represents the best and the brightest the church has to offer.

But Susan found greater acceptance of her leadership gifts in commerce than in the community of God. She discovered a radical acceptance outside the church that she couldn't find inside it. The church lost her. We not only lost her allegiance, we lost her attention. Now we're not even important enough to be mad at.

Fast Facts

71% say I have no (39 percent) or not too much (32 percent) fear in my spiritual life these days.

69% say The media has no (25 percent) or not much (44 percent) influence on my life decisions.

1% say I constantly (0.5 percent) or pretty often (0.5 percent) struggle with jealousy.

Our Bloggers Said

If you had asked me these questions ten years ago, I would probably have answered that I never have a spirit of fear, I'm never jealous of anyone, and the media had little influence on me, and it would have been a *pack* of lies. But I was trying so hard to wear the right mask and fit in. I didn't want anyone to see the chinks in the armor I'd so carefully crafted.

■ ■ ■

I do experience the temptation to be jealous of the women/people in church leadership, or the marriages that seem perfect in areas where mine is struggling. But I've learned that appearances can be deceiving and that we all struggle in different ways. As soon as the thought comes into my head, I cast it down and realize that's just a "wile" of the devil. So honestly, I could classify myself as someone who doesn't experience jealousy.

■ ■ ■

When mainstream evangelical Christian media voices talk about "the media," they are almost without exception speaking in negative tones about the immorality or "bad" politics promoted there. So when Christians hear this and then question whether "the media" has affected their decisions, they are well trained to think, *No, I'm not like "the media," because I hold different values and beliefs. My decisions are influenced by my faith, my church, and my family.* Sorry folks, but you're just not as objective as you might think.

Re-Signed
They Wouldn't Take No for an Answer

Kelly and Sadell won't leave and they won't quit. They've learned the art of defining themselves and staying connected. They're engaged but not owned; integrated within the church but knowledgeable about its inherent limitations and dangers. They've discovered ways to contribute to something they've accepted they cannot change, and they won't be deterred, regardless of the number of barriers put in front of them. They have found creative workarounds that provide them with enough spiritual breathing room to bring their best leadership to the churches they love. These women are veterans who have re-signed up on their own terms.

CHAPTER 14

YOU DON'T NEED PERMISSION

The Kelly Bean Story

As I MENTIONED, my mom, my sister, and my wife are all leaders, and even my first pastor was a woman.

So compared to many men, I'm decidedly pro-women. And from the time Off The Map began over ten years ago, I talked about the importance of women leading. I supported them and defended their right to have as much influence as any man. But sadly my actions weren't reflecting my rhetoric: in Off The Map's early days, you wouldn't have found many women at our board meetings or on our stage.

So when I went looking for a new member of our board of directors, I knew it had to be a woman. That's when a pastor friend of mine told me, "You need to meet Kelly Bean."

Turns out I'd already met Kelly. In 2001, Off The Map

put on our first national conference. Before it began, we gave the attendees some homework. We asked them to ask as many non-Christians as possible this question: "If you thought Christians would listen, what would you tell them?" Kelly Bean collected more responses than anyone else. I knew she instinctively understood what Off The Map was about. She "got" our love for the people Jesus misses most. She was a practitioner, a doer. So after she was recommended to me, I invited her to be on our board of directors, and she served in that capacity for several years.

Kelly and her husband, Ken, have three kids and one grandchild. They've been married for over twenty-five years. Kelly is the oldest of four girls and by her own admission was "a very shy and reflective kid." Growing up, her family attended a traditional mainline church.

Unlike Kelly, I wasn't raised in church, but many of my friends were. And through my conversations with them, I've come to recognize the powerful role their early childhood church experiences had on them, for better or sometimes worse. So I asked Kelly how her early church experience influenced her life. "I spent most of my time analyzing hymns. I love hymns, but for some reason I never really 'bought in' to what they were talking about from the pulpit, which I guess has continued to be a practice that's both served me and complicated my life."

Kelly's grandfather was a minister and her dad was very active in the church or, as Kelly puts it, "My dad was a Christian *and* a religious addict."

It has never ceased to amaze me how so many people become Christians *in spite of* their spiritual role models' influence. I asked Kelly to explain to me how God was able to earn her trust even though her father violated it.

"He talked to me."

"Talked to you?"

"Yes, when I was ten years old, God talked to me."

"Audibly?"

"Yes, I was just drifting off to sleep when I heard a voice calling my name. It was a deep voice, so I thought it might be my dad. I got up, went downstairs, and asked my dad if he wanted something. He said no, so I trundled back upstairs, lay down, and tried to go back to sleep, only to be awakened again by the same voice saying, *Be baptized*. I knew it was God. The next morning I informed my mom that God had personally instructed me to be baptized. She was shocked since she knew how fearful I was of the water—particularly of putting my head under. But she talked with the pastor, and within a couple of weeks I marched into the baptistery and obeyed what God had told me to do."

I know how skeptical I am when people tell me they've heard directly from God, so I wondered how Kelly's mom and pastor interpreted her encounter with him. "Do you think your mom and your pastor believed that you actually heard God's voice?"

"I think my mom really believed me," Kelly said. "Her example of kindness and faith has been such an important factor in my choosing to follow Jesus over the years. And the pastor? Well, my hunch is that he just sort of overlooked how I got there and baptized me. As I got older I figured out that I shouldn't tell that story, so I kept it to myself and only told people who I thought would get it."

Kelly's "as I got older" comment triggered something in me. Why of all people do Christians find it necessary to hide who they really are? Where do we see Jesus encouraging this dehumanizing practice? While researching for this book, I've discovered that women seem especially attuned to the need to hide their real thoughts and feelings.

Kelly had that look in her eye that told me she had something to add. "I think it's because so often women aren't welcome to express who they really are and what they feel God's called them to be."

My conversation with Kelly had shifted to something more than just the recollection of a childhood memory. I heard a tone in her voice that suggested she felt pain over this exclusion even in her adulthood.

When Ken and Kelly were first married, they attended a charismatic church in Portland. A dynamic woman named Jane led the Sunday school. As you probably know, most Sunday school classes can never get enough volunteers, but apparently Jane's had a waiting list. "People were attracted by her obvious leadership gift. Although Jane wasn't officially approved to be *in the ministry*, she was given permission to hold a midweek service for the volunteers who worked for her on Sunday and had to miss church. Of course, this meeting was not considered to be an *official* church service because that would have meant Jane was a pastor."

"Was she on staff or a volunteer?" I asked.

"She was paid staff," said Kelly. "But at some point Jane discovered that her male colleagues—including the youth pastor—were being paid nearly twice as much as what she made. Their rationale was that men were the breadwinners, so they had to be paid more. Jane's husband was expected to provide for their income needs."

What Kelly was describing is the power distance index, a term popularized by Malcolm Gladwell.[1] Essentially, the PDI informs how people relate to each other around power. Cultures with a high PDI expect and accept that power is distributed unequally. Those with a lower rank are discouraged from speaking up or expecting equal treatment. I explained this to Kelly, telling her that it sounded to me like church communities have their own PDI, especially when it comes to how men and women relate to each other. Kelly listened intently, then responded. "The sad irony is that this particular denomination was already ordaining women as pastors."

I've known Kelly and her husband for a number of years. It was difficult for me to imagine this sophisticated, free-spirited couple settling into a church community that treated women this way. "How do you think your church's viewpoint affected your marriage?" I asked.

"We were a product of the times," answered Kelly, "so Ken attempted to go along with the man-as-the-head-of-the-house deal, but behind closed doors we were actually a very egalitarian household. We've always charted our course together, though Ken likes to say he'll follow me anywhere!"

I asked Kelly where she found the courage to differentiate herself as a leader and what kept her from walking away from church.

"I read a book by Madeleine L'Engle, an Episcopalian. Her story gave me hope for a way to go forward with the church. But let me tell you more about what happened after Ken and I left that church."

Kelly explained that her husband had a close friend who was planting a nondenominational church, and he asked them to join it. Knowing that this friend held a traditional view of the role of women in the church, Kelly was reluctant. Eventually, though, she relented and they started to attend. Then Ken was asked to be an elder.

"He said yes, hoping he could change things," says Kelly. "At home he would seek my counsel about church decisions. This was a perfect setup since I wasn't invited but still had opinions. After getting my feedback secondhand through my husband, the pastor began talking with me 'off the record,' and I became something of a spiritual adviser to him. He appeared to be pretty open to my ideas and even seemed open to modifying his traditional view of the role of women in the church.

"At one point he invited everyone in the church to research the issue of women in ministry and present a paper to the rest of the congregation. I was surprised when I was the only one in the church who took him up on the offer.

After my paper was read at the appointed meeting, the pastor made it quite clear he didn't agree with my position, though it was obvious many there did. In fact, he refused to speak with me except when necessary for the next several months."

Kelly's pastor's response was certainly insensitive, but it was not all that unusual. Kelly was experiencing what I call the "background singers" phenomenon. Background singers have access to the stage *as long as they stay out of the spotlight.*

In a similar way, many pastors have learned how to use women's leadership gifts while simultaneously refusing them the title of leader. I've spent forty years observing and being one of the people paid to be Christians and have concluded that many pastors have gotten stuck in this dishonest dance. They depend upon women's spiritual insights to help the church grow while reserving the right to refuse them access to the main stage.

Despite the cold response from their pastor, Kelly and Ken remained actively involved there for several more years. Eventually, though, they decided to part ways with that church.

I wanted to know more. "So what happened after that? How did you manage to continue to grow as a leader?"

Because of her desire to advance a more inclusive approach to Christianity, Kelly said she attended an early meeting held by an emergent church network in 2002. "It was thought provoking and inspiring," she says, "but—when it came to advancing women as leaders—it was still more of the same."

I told Kelly that my organization, Off The Map, hadn't been any better when it began. Unfortunately, we had become good at giving women just enough stage time to *appear* as if we cared. As I mentioned early in the book, I have never forgotten my friend Rose's analysis after one of our events: "You tried, but you failed."

Nevertheless, like all great leaders Kelly was able to regroup and move forward.

"I became friends with Brian McLaren and his wife, Grace. Over the years they've opened doors for me, demonstrated respect for my leadership, and encouraged me along the way. They introduced me to a much wider network. It was that association that ultimately inspired me to start Convergence, a network for women to connect with and empower each other."

I told Kelly that from my vantage point many women's networks connect women, but when it comes to developing women leaders, they hold back. She told me that Convergence is different.

"We're not on a mission to overthrow pastors or the church. We're on a mission to empower and connect women who follow Jesus and want to advance his Kingdom. We're creating a cross-denominational network of support to encourage women as leaders."

Kelly has definitely earned the right to lead. She's paid her dues. For more than twenty years, she's been leading a spiritual community that began when she and Ken were part of other churches. Ironically, while all of those churches have come and gone, her little church has continued. She's quite passionate about and committed to her community.

"Twenty-four years ago we started a home group that met weekly for sixteen years. We now meet once each month for an extended afternoon and evening. It's where I learned to lead, and it's where no one could put limits on me. This is my church and I love it. It's a community I cultivate and pastor.

"Followers of Jesus will naturally find a connection within a community, but what that looks like will vary," Kelly says. "Just because people gather in a building, it does not necessarily equal community or church. Going to church isn't the point; *being* the church is."

• • •

My Take

One of my hopes as I wrote this book was that while reading the stories you would feel uncomfortable at least once. That's how you know you're growing.

Here's what I wonder: Why did Kelly feel she had to start her own church? Do we really want gifted leaders like her wasting their valuable time "working around men"? Think about all the energy Kelly spent trying to "guess" what her pastor would or wouldn't approve of. Men sometimes accuse women of being indirect in order to get their way. We jokingly refer to it as "the neck that turns the head," meaning as long as it appears women aren't actually leading, we'll let them do the work. We'll give them responsibility but not authority. Can you imagine Jesus doing that?

As long as the currently popular idea of indirect influence being the acceptable norm for women prevails, we should expect to see more women follow in Kelly's footsteps and simply bypass asking permission. I, for one, salute them.

CHAPTER 15

A PRAGMATIC WOMAN

The Sadell Bradley Story

THE INDIE MUSIC, vintage furniture, and low lights provided a great vibe for a group of about twenty-five church leaders who had gathered at the Speckled Bird Café in the gritty neighborhood of Norwood, Ohio. We were there to discuss the pros and cons of the missional movement—the desire to live on mission for God's Kingdom as biblically faithful and contextualized congregations. I was enjoying the participation and the way the discussion was heading . . . and then Sadell spoke.

"May I ask a question?" All eyes turned to her. (When Sadell said this, it was more like she was making an announcement than posing a question.)

"What does missional mean to people like me?" she said. "I mean, I appreciate all of you wanting to be helpful, do more social justice, and reach out to the marginalized, but did any of you notice that my husband, Sherman, and I are the only two black people in this room?"

I immediately liked Sadell. She was a take-no-prisoners kind of woman. Even better, she was willing to help white people "get it" if we were willing to listen.

She continued making us uncomfortable.

"How can this be God's idea when there's almost zero diversity in the room? Isn't this just a newer, hipper version of what already exists in the church?"

Sadell spoke with a sly smile and sparkling eyes. She conveyed confidence without a hint of condescension, superiority, or anger in her voice. She was simply telling it like it was for anyone who was willing to listen.

When I interviewed her later, Sadell told me she doesn't know who her dad is and never met her birth mom. During her first three years, she was shifted between a Catholic girls home and foster care. At age three, she was adopted by a young single African American schoolteacher who lived with her older sister and their father.

"My adoptive mother was the first in our family to graduate from college with a combination math, music, and education degree," Sadell says. Adopting Sadell was a brave move. "She wore a ring on her left hand to pretend she was married to avoid being judged for having a daughter," she says.

"My adoptive grandmother was also a teacher in the

South, but she did not have a college degree. When my grandmother moved from Virginia to Pennsylvania, she had to work as a domestic [housekeeper]. During the Depression, my mother and aunt joined her and worked in white people's houses. Eventually, through much sacrifice, my family pitched in to see that my mother attended and graduated from Hampton University [then Hampton Institute], where Booker T. Washington went to school."

This threesome—her adoptive mother, aunt, and grandfather—became Sadell's nuclear family. She was an only child, and they lavished love and attention on her accordingly. It was through their influence that Sadell first encountered God.

"Somewhere around the time of my adoption I began to have a sense of God—that I was on earth to serve his purposes. As an adopted person, I felt as if I had no origin. Life felt ambiguous—like a vapor. As a child, I was taught that I got here through the divine providence of God and that my birth mother, like Moses' mother, was a conduit for the path God had predestined for me. This story grounded and stabilized me."

Sadell was raised in the local "black" church, where her family members were prominent church members. Whenever the doors were open, they were there. Sadell found her musical voice early on.

"I was a part of a local singing group, and we had to follow a strict biblical code of conduct and dress, particularly the women," she recalled. "Girls were not allowed to wear pants, jewelry, braids, or makeup. This was done in obedience to Scriptures such as Deuteronomy 22:5 (KJV): 'The woman shall not wear that which pertaineth unto a man, neither shall a man put on a woman's garment: for all that do so are abomination unto the LORD thy God' and 1 Peter 3:3 (KJV): 'Whose adorning let it not be that outward adorning of plaiting the hair, and of wearing of gold, or of putting on of apparel.'

"I found it amusing and confusing, however, that the singing group supervisor who enforced the dress code for women also coached the church's track team, whose members were permitted to wear shorts and sleeveless tank tops."

Sadell's ability to spot such disconnects and her intensity toward mission have made her a valuable member of many church groups. I asked her to list the various ways she has served in the church.

After starting out in the children's and youth choirs, she became a youth leader and served as a national youth leader for a choral convention. She has always been very active in music ministry, serving as a background singer for Christian artists, worship director, music director, and music pastor. She has also been a church elder, itinerant minister, leader in her church's singles' and women's ministry, and missionary, both on a college campus and to Africa.

"I've also cleaned the church, decorated the church, planned events, done secretarial work, run the sound and audiovisual, written curriculum, written policy and procedure manuals, evangelized, served communion, done nursing home ministry, visited the sick, preached and sung in the prison, and taught welfare-to-work courses for the homeless, formerly incarcerated, and drug addicted," she said.

After college, Sadell moved to Ohio, where she joined a church that was starting to open up to the Spirit as well as to provide more freedom for women.

"Unbeknownst to me," she says, "this church was undergoing a spiritual revival of sorts and was about to drop its denominational ties. Everything was changing in the heart and mind of the pastor, including his view on the role of women. Prior to this movement of the Spirit, he was strictly against women ministers. The Lord moved in his heart, and after much study he became convinced that he needed to bring women into the forefront. I was one of the first women leaders he asked to be an elder.

"Because of my own questions around the gender issue and the fear that if I accepted this role I might never end up getting married, I said no. To be honest, I actually thought, *I'm only being asked because some man is refusing his call.* However, a few years later, after much urging by the Lord, I relented and accepted the role of elder and pastor of music, worship, and the arts. I was one of four women pastors on staff at that time. We were quite a spectacle at the local pastors' meetings—where it was understood we were not to speak even though at 'home' we had the full endorsement of our senior pastor. In fact, he would often challenge the congregation to measure our impact against any man and then tell him why we should not be leading."

I wondered how Sadell could tell that her pastor really valued her leadership. What did he do that assured her that she was not seen merely as a token?

"Jim," she told me, "there were three important things my pastor did that told me he was for real. Number one, he personally acknowledged and called out my gift of leadership. Two, he paid me—not a lot, but enough to show me he respected me. Number three, he gave me authority to directly lead almost two hundred people—which is a number larger than most American churches—in addition to teaching and leading the congregation in worship, and he did not micromanage me. I ended up working on staff with his church for fourteen years."

Sadell recently accepted possibly her most challenging ministry assignment to date. For the past few years, she and Sherman have been attending a Pentecostal church that is committed to racial reconciliation in keeping with its denomination's beginnings. The Azusa Street Revival (1906–1915) that birthed the Pentecostal movement was a phenomenon in part because of its diversity and the leadership of William J. Seymour, an African American pastor whose parents were former slaves. After the revival, the churches split along racial lines to become various Pentecostal denominations. A movement is now underway to reconcile the racial divide.

"To be honest, in the past racial diversity in the church wasn't a front-burner issue for me," Sadell admitted. "I didn't see it happening in the churches I attended. In fact, one of the fears I heard from some pastors in the black church over the radio was that if too many white people got involved, they would take over one of the few remaining bastions of black empowerment. However, God has made it clear to me that *he* is interested in unity and reconciliation, so I will be too."

Sadell said she now serves as a bridge builder in systems that have had very few women or black people in positions of visible leadership. Her pastor, a longtime friend, is white and extremely committed to racial and economic reconciliation as well as social justice.

In addition to her worship and teaching ministry, Sadell serves as a campus missionary for Chi Alpha Christian Fellowship, a campus ministry sponsored by the Assemblies of God. She is currently the only African American woman serving as a Chi Alpha missionary in the state and one of only a few in the nation. She has to raise her own financial support, something that is generally not practiced in the black church.

"Even though I'm the official campus missionary, I like to pull Sherman in to fly cover for me. The church at large is still pretty traditional about the gender issue, so having my husband along helps smooth the way in terms of getting a hearing, as well as raising money. Some women may see this as me riding a man's coattails, but I am accustomed to operating under a senior pastor's covering. I'm used to having a man in that role, and frankly I prefer it—not because I feel inadequate but because I'm willing to do whatever it takes to 'get 'er done.'

"I've been in significant leadership for over twenty years now, Jim, but I didn't really seek it because I anticipated the problems and really wanted no part of them. It wasn't that I didn't want to serve the Lord or the church; I just didn't want the foolishness. I've closely observed the pressure key leaders experience as a result of bearing that kind of responsibility. That's what influences my desire to work in shared leadership, either with my husband or another male leader. Women benefit from men who advocate for them in the same way African Americans benefit from white people who open doors for them."

Sadell's mother remains perhaps the most influential person in her life. Sadell told me that when President Obama was elected, she especially wanted to talk with her mom to get her historical perspective.

"I said, 'Mom, you lived through the Depression, World War II, Jim Crow laws, segregation, the women's liberation movement, and the civil rights movement. You even adopted me as a single parent when it was unpopular to do so. So I don't need to listen to other people's views on the significance of this election. I can get my insight from you!' I look at my mother and see a woman of strength, brilliance, and character. I would be thrilled if I were able to become half the woman she is. Because of her example, there is little that I believe women cannot do.

"And while my position on this issue may disappoint some," Sadell said, "I continue to believe in the scriptural headship of a man in the family relationship and that the soundness of that union will, in most instances, be reflected in local church leadership. But it seems to me that there is an expectation from God that men and women can and should 'have dominion' together. I look at the pastors/apostles Priscilla and Aquila as an example of this. I do think various interpretations of certain Scriptures have led to unfortunate division in the Christian community. Sometimes they have been misinterpreted to the males' advantage because no one took the time or was inclined to look at the cultural context."

• • •

My Take

I finished this interview and realized I didn't have a category for Sadell. Her pragmatism was startling. I find her thinking to be fascinating and revealing when it comes to navigating the twists and turns around power and those who hold it. If you're like me, there were times in her story that you started to settle in and feel as if you'd gotten a handle on her, and then whooom—she made a sudden right turn. You found yourself desperately wanting out of her car.

Despite her willingness to let men take the lead, Sadell is one of the strongest women I met on my interview tour. One of the attributes I love most about her is her commitment to "keeping it real"—even when she made me uncomfortable. I wish there wasn't a black church and a white church. I find explaining that distinction to non-believers difficult and embarrassing.

As we learned in her story, Sadell operates in the mostly seg-regated American church that's also still undecided about the level of influence they think women should have. Consider the fact that Sadell is an African American woman, and you begin to appreciate the complex set of circumstances she has to negotiate. That's why Sadell doesn't care what you and I think of her . . . quite frankly she can't afford to care.

Fast Facts

82% say I agree strongly (55 percent) or somewhat (27 percent) that I can tell by its actions that my church values the leadership of women as much as it values the leadership of men.

Our Bloggers Said

My first encounter with the "issue" of women in positions of power in the church, namely teaching and pastorate roles, was in college. For a project, I was required to call my home church and ask what the official stance on women was. At the time, I would have answered exactly like the women in the above stats. So when I heard my pastor say women were not allowed to teach men, or pastor, I was shocked. I look back now and wonder how I could have assumed otherwise . . . but here is the thing, it was never overtly stated . . . ever. Instead it was a very quiet, subtle thing. Women never stood at the pulpit; women were not elders. I was never presented with the possibility of seminary for my future. I was never encouraged to use my gifts in ministry.

■ ■ ■

One of the very subtle ways the church trains women is to make us think, from a very young age, that serving is the noblest of calls. We are to stand behind the men in leadership, knowing that they couldn't do it without us. We are to be proud of taking a lesser role. And if you don't want to do that, then you are sinning against God with pride and lust for power. Again, all this [is] taught very subtly. I think this may contribute to why women lash out against those who try to break free of this. We were taught it was sin.

■ ■ ■

In my experience evangelical churches and seminaries are still bastions of male dominated leadership and teaching. Sure, many pastors "say" they promote women in leadership, but in action women aren't the ones who get to preach or get hired for leadership roles. Further, doctrines can still be heard relating the ills of church to women not submitting to men.

■ ■ ■

My own views of women in the church have changed/ formed in the last few years as my local congregation has opened all roles to women, including elder and pastor. Our denomination allows each congregation to make this determination, and there are many who do not allow it. My pastor is definitely supportive of women in leadership, and was very encouraging to me particularly as I recently began a term as a deacon in my church.

■ ■ ■

At least one reason I have pursued a career in academia is because of my inability to find a hospitable place to serve in a preaching/pastoring capacity within the local church (at least, in my own evangelical tradition). So, as far as I'm concerned, you can probably count me among those women who have already "left the building" due to the limitations of traditional evangelical churches.

Re-Signed
They Won't Take No for an Answer

Innovative people always face resistance. Innovative women seem to face it even more. Take Denie and Jennifer, for example. Listen to their stories and ask yourself, *Why didn't these women walk away? What makes them tick? What part of "no" don't they understand?*

CHAPTER 16

SANDWICH LADY MEETS MEN OF GOD

The Denie Tackett Story

PAM HOGEWEIDE IS A great writer. She was also my guide and second set of eyes on this project. Pam connected me to a number of innovative, Kingdom-advancing women who won't take no for an answer, even when it comes from a man. She told me about her friend Denie and encouraged me to include her story in this book.

Denie and Pam have been friends for many years. They met in Sin City as teenagers. Pam was native to Las Vegas, but Denie moved there during high school. After meeting each other at the same summer job, they became friends instantly.

One of Pam's fondest memories is of the two of them jetting around the Strip in Denie's '67 chocolate brown Mustang with Foghat rocking full blast on the eight track. Picture a younger version of Thelma and Louise, road-tripping on the neon-soaked boulevards of Vegas, and you'd have Pam and Denie.

Along with hundreds of other young people, Denie and Pam spent hours at the top of Sahara Boulevard on the west side of the Vegas valley. The view of glimmering lights from the hotels and casinos resembled a sea of sparkly jewels. The boulevard was a great place for teenagers to party, as long as the cops didn't show up.

The teens' hangout also was a place for the two girls to get away from their rocky home lives. Getting high was another form of escape. In fact, they took their first acid trip together at the top of Sahara.

Then one day Denie and Pam decided to run away together. Denie didn't want to take the Mustang because the registration had her dad's name on it. So they packed up their stuff and began riding the bus all over the city. They landed on the wrong side of town while trying to find the apartment of some friends, where they hoped to crash until they had figured out their next step. There was only one problem: they couldn't remember where the apartment was located.

As they sat in front of a convenience store, a pretty, experienced-looking blonde approached Denie and Pam.

"Are you guys running away?" she asked.

"No," said Denie. "We're just traveling around." Pam stared at her friend, impressed with her street smarts.

"That's cool," said the blonde. "I did some of that when I

was younger too. But, hey, you guys shouldn't be around here. This is a real bad neighborhood, and a couple of young girls like you could get hurt. Let me give you a ride out of here."

Grateful for her offer, they climbed into her beat-up car. She dropped them off at an intersection they thought might be near the apartment.

It never worked out. They walked until late that night. Pam finally said, "Hey, I'm going home." Denie crashed at the house of some other people she knew.

Denie never went home again.

She and Pam eventually lost touch. Then Pam's whole life changed after she attended a Christian concert in downtown Las Vegas. Unexpectedly she decided to follow Christ. She was a bona fide Jesus freak! No more sex, drugs, or rock 'n' roll.

Out of the blue, Denie began calling Pam. She told Pam she had gotten married, had kids, and moved with her family to Florida. Pam told her friend how Jesus had changed her life. Denie would listen and cry softly as Pam explained the gospel to her. Not long after this—with an assist from some door-knocking Baptists—Denie gave her life to Christ too. Her decision to follow Jesus brought the two young women even closer together and revitalized their friendship.

Eventually Pam, her husband, Jerry, and their kids settled in Portland. After a divorce Denie moved with her three boys to Boise. Pam and Denie stayed in touch with the occasional card or call. But it was Denie's phone call telling Pam that she wanted to minister to the homeless that got the two friends talking more often.

"Pam, I've been praying about it, and I think I'm supposed to minister to the homeless," Denie told her friend one day. "I'm going to start helping out at one of the shelters."

A few months later, though, Denie called Pam to tell her she'd already quit. "It's just too institutionalized, Pam. I think I'll just go down to the park and hand out sandwiches myself."

Denie started by simply walking around a park near downtown Boise where she knew homeless people congregated. Her plan was pretty simple: load up a tote bag with water bottles and bologna sandwiches and pass them out at the park.

But like a first-timer in a karaoke bar, once she got there she got stage fright. "Pam, that first time I was so scared," she told her friend. "I couldn't get out of my truck. I was shaking and praying, 'God, are you sure this is what I'm supposed to do?'" After saying a few more prayers, she stepped out of her truck and began to hand out the food and water. She was relieved that no one threatened her or yelled at her.

Denie went back the next week, and the week after that, and the week after that. Soon she was telling her church about her efforts to serve the homeless men and women of Boise. Their response: "Why don't you just invite them to come to church instead?"

Denie tried to imagine how that would work. She pictured Merlin, an alcoholic who smelled of urine and stale smoke, stepping into the beautifully carpeted sanctuary of the church. *Um, nope, that probably wouldn't work out too well,* she decided. Though her church family appeared concerned about her ministry, Denie grew more comfortable in her role and continued to pass out water and sandwiches to her new friends "without homes."

Then the woman issue began to surface. The first one to bring it up was another concerned woman who actually told Denie that she was a loose woman for going alone to minister to men and that, as a single woman, she should be involved in the church ministries and looking for a husband. Denie was beginning to learn that even if all a woman is doing is serving water and bologna sandwiches, if it's called a ministry, the church has a different set of rules for women than for men. "There had been other times I felt God tugging me to ministry," Denie told Pam, "but I ignored those tugs because being a single divorced woman and only seeing men preaching, the church implied that as a woman, I was a nobody. I was here to serve the church and leave the ministering to the men."

Denie was shocked and hurt at this insult and eventually left that church. The lack of support for her ministry to the homeless was just too discouraging. But as it turns out, that would be the least of the challenges Denie would face in her attempts to deliver food and water to homeless people. As Denie's reputation as "the Sandwich Lady" grew, other street ministers began to flock to the park. One of those ministers was particularly vocal about his beliefs about women in ministry. "A woman shouldn't do what you're doing. Women are meant to be helpmates to men," he told her. And if that wasn't insulting enough, "this same guy had the nerve to introduce me to one of his friends as 'his disciple,'" Denie said.

One man suggested that Denie let him lead the park ministry. "He said that since I was a woman, I needed to come under his leadership like a wife comes under her husband's. He felt that it was the man's place to lead, but that I could help and serve," said Denie. "At that moment it hit me. As a woman, he viewed my only purpose in life as serving men. Apparently in his eyes, women couldn't hold a position of authority."

Denie had never thought much about her beliefs concerning women and leadership. She was just doing what God asked her to do. And she was making inroads into the lives of some of the most severely broken men and women in her city. One woman wouldn't even look at Denie for months; then one day, she finally accepted a sandwich and bottle of water. She had begun to trust Denie and soon began confiding in her. Just as a missionary in Papua New Guinea might do, Denie had been humbly paying her dues to reach this hard-core tribe of overlooked people.

But as much as Denie loved her homeless friends, the weight of shouldering such responsibility began to take its toll. She was no longer just handing out water and bologna sandwiches; she was also trying to engage in a host of new relationships. Every day Denie would receive pleas for help. Some people needed a ride to the hospital or to a social service appointment. Many people called just to chat. Denie found herself spending more and more time hanging out with her friends from the park.

Denie knew she needed help, but she didn't know where to turn or whom to ask. Several people had come alongside Denie to help on Saturdays. Her son, James, for instance, was a huge help loading and unloading Denie's truck. What she really needed was someone to help colead. But who?

Pam noticed that Denie sounded increasingly tired over the phone. "You need partners, Denie. It's gotten too big for you to do alone anymore," she told her.

Sometimes Pam and Denie talked about the possibility of Denie quitting her ministry. "Maybe I'll pack up and move to Portland," Denie told Pam. "I can help Ken with HOMEpdx."

Ken Loyd, a close friend of Pam's, has a street church. Ken does in Portland what Denie does in Boise. But Ken is a man and a pastor, and he has coleaders and teams helping him serve the homeless.

Concerned for her friend's emotional well-being, Pam introduced Denie to another friend of hers named Vivian, who also worked with homeless people in Portland. *If nothing else,* Pam thought, *Vivian might at least be able to offer Denie some moral support.*

Vivian, a petite, dark-haired woman with black ink tattoos on her arms, had moved to Portland from Southern California. She was one of the people who helped launch HOMEpdx with Ken.

Denie connected easily with Vivian. The two became fast friends during a trip to Portland. After that, they kept in touch through e-mails.

Vivian had other close friends in Boise, people she knew from her faith community in Southern California. It didn't take long for her to connect Denie to these people, and it wasn't long before Vivian's friends were affected by Denie's passion for feeding the homeless in the park. Was God up to something?

Vivian's friends Todd and Debbie Hunter had moved to Boise from Southern California a few years earlier. Todd is the former national director of the Vineyard Churches and the former president of Alpha USA. He now serves as the bishop for the West Coast Province of the Anglican Mission in the Americas. With those kinds of credentials, it's no surprise that Denie assumed Todd would be the last person interested in helping her serve water and sandwiches to the homeless.

"Here was this bigwig," recalls Denie, "asking questions and writing checks to help me buy supplies. I kept my guard up. Since he was a man with an impressive résumé, I figured it was only a matter of time before he'd tell me, 'Step aside, little lady, and let me show you how this is really supposed to be done.'" Little did she know that was the last thing Todd wanted.

As Todd and his community began to come to the park, a new kind of challenge to Denie's leadership emerged. But this time it didn't come from a man; it came from within herself. Doubts about her leadership that lurked just beneath the surface were eating away at her confidence.

"I was sitting in a restaurant with Todd and Debbie and

decided to be up-front with them," she told Pam. "I poured out my frustrations and fears regarding my lack of qualifications. I needed to know how they felt about those issues and how they felt about me.

"Reaching across the table, Todd touched my hand and looked me straight in the eye as he said, 'You are who God made you, Denie, and Debbie and I are with you 100 percent.'" For the first time, Denie was experiencing true collaboration in ministry with a male colleague.

"When I walk into the room, Todd and I are equals. We're working together. No one is better than anyone else because of education or gender. There's mutual respect," says Denie. "For example, when we recently talked about a conflict occurring during our park visits, Todd spoke with me as a coleader, not a boss. He is one of the few men I know who treats me as a fellow minister. He accepts me and honors my God-given calling."

Not long ago, Pam went with Vivian to Boise to spend time with Denie and the Hunters. A hub of activity buzzed around the Hunters' kitchen as Debbie prepared huge pots of pasta and meatballs with tomato sauce for the following day at the park.

As Pam and Denie sat together at their dining room table, Denie leaned over to her friend and whispered, "Pam, Todd told me I'm his hero!" Pam responded, "Right on!" Todd had given Denie acceptance and respect, which was all she really needed to keep going to the park to hang out with her friends without homes.

I think Denie is a hero, too, but not just because she serves bologna sandwiches to people without homes. Denie is a hero because of her willingness to keep following Jesus in spite of the confusing messages she has received from churches, street preachers, men, and women.

• • •

My Take

Can you imagine Jesus telling a woman that in order to qualify as someone who could feed homeless people bologna sandwiches, she first needed to find a man to submit her ministry to? Seriously, out of what school of thought does this crazy-making, Kingdom-stopping, egocentric rationale emerge? Certainly not from the Jesus school of disciple making.

The contrast between how Denie was treated by the preachers in the park and how she was treated by Todd and Debbie is night and day. One group sought power; the other gave power. Denie's struggle is not a gender issue, it's a power issue. Until those with power (men) decide to give it away to those who lack it (women), I believe we will continue to misrepresent Jesus' heart and mar the beauty of his Kingdom.

CHAPTER 17

DEEP RESILIENCE

The Jennifer Roach Story

NODAL EVENTS, like breaking up with one's first boyfriend or girlfriend, winning the lottery, or losing a parent to divorce or death, are experiences that are flash frozen on our psyches; they're circumstantial tipping points.

That's what happened to Jennifer when she was just twelve years old. Her family lived in central California, but then her dad landed a new job with General Foods in Princeton, New Jersey. He moved ahead of the family to get a house and make other preparations.

Now thirty-nine, married, and a mom, Jennifer told me the story in a matter-of-fact tone as only an adult is capable of doing, although by the look in her eyes I sensed that her twelve-year-old self was lurking nearby.

"My dad was killed in a car accident while he was getting ready to move the family to New Jersey," she said.

Jen was part of a typical seventies nuclear family. Mom, dad, three kids. She's in the middle. Her older sister reacted to her father's tragic death by rebelling, but Jen became the good girl.

"I loved going to church," she recalls. "If there was any possibility of my being there, I'd be there."

In California, Jen's family attended a large, seeker-sensitive church. As in many families, Jen's mom took the kids to church, but her dad had gone only when he needed to be there for one of their activities.

Jen dove into the church experience and made it her surrogate family.

"I loved my Sunday school teacher, Mrs. Honeycutt. She and Mr. Honeycutt told stories about missionaries around the world, and I was riveted. I remember pretending to be a Bible translator. I created my own imaginary tribe and language, which I wrote out on three-by-five-inch cards. The Honeycutts rewarded my spiritual curiosity and leadership with attention and encouragement. I've never forgotten them."

By the time Jen was fifteen, it was clear her family would never return to normal. Her mom had gone back to work, and their home seemed to get smaller as the three kids got older. The rest of her family had dropped out of church, but Jen was spending more and more time involved in church activities. Sensing her family's predicament, Jen's youth pastor reached out to her and her mom, inviting Jen to live with him and his wife until things could get worked out at home.

"It only took three weeks," Jen said, sounding as calm as a news anchor on the local six o'clock broadcast.

As we sat in the coffee shop for her interview, Seattle traffic whizzing by, people continued ordering their lattes and tapping on their iPhones and laptops. Jen's words, however, stopped me.

Sensing bad news, I asked, "He came after you sexually?"

"Yes, but not directly. He started with inappropriate touching. He would immediately apologize and say it wouldn't happen again, but it did."

Awkwardly I asked, "How personal did this get, Jen?"

"Very, very personal, Jim."

As a dad with two daughters of my own—both of whom are Jen's age—I felt sick and incredibly angry.

"That's statutory rape!" I said loudly.

This guy had groomed Jen; he was a predator. He saw a mark and went after her. She was vulnerable—no dad and a depressed mom. No one could protect her. This arrangement had continued undetected for two more years.

Amazed I asked, "How did you guys hide this from his wife?"

"There was only one car, and he knew when she would be coming home." Once they even went together to a seminar on youth conflict. During breaks, they went to his car and made out. "Another time," Jen said, "he saw me sitting on a boy's lap at youth group and told me that was 'an inappropriate way for a Christian girl to be with a boy.'"

Jen didn't out the youth pastor. "I thought of him as a father figure and always hoped we could have a normal friendship." He eventually moved away and took a job in another church in Canada. His wife never suspected anything.

At age seventeen, Jen read *Macbeth* in high school, which somehow inspired her to talk. She met with her pastors and told them the whole story.

"Two men interviewed me; no women were present. They asked specific questions. I was humiliated."

I asked Jen if the pastors told her to talk to her mom or arranged a meeting for her with their wives.

"No, they told me it would be best for me if I kept this quiet. I begged them not to tell my mother. It was as if we made a trade-off and both stuck to the agreement."

The pastors did call their ex–youth pastor and gave him a week to tell his wife. If he didn't, they said, they would tell her for him. That was the only discipline he received at that time.

Jen served faithfully in that church for another five years. "I was hopeful that someone would eventually point me in the right direction to find help overcoming that experience."

No pastor (or pastor's wife) ever came to talk with her again, no one arranged counseling, and her mother was never told about the criminal activity of the predatory youth pastor. Jen's personal life didn't seem to be coming together either. She could barely make ends meet on her part-time wages as a day-care worker. Attempts at community college were just as bad. "Getting from bed to class was incredibly difficult," Jen explained.

Jen was left with the impression that whenever the church offered protection, it always came with a price tag attached. The youth pastor provided a perverted form of acceptance in exchange for her body, and the two other male pastors promised to keep her secret in exchange for her silence.

Still, Jen continued to embrace the faith of those who had abused and used her. She continued to aspire to serve Jesus and influence others to follow him, but she intuitively understood that she needed a man to open the doors for her.

"I eventually left my big church for a smaller church that was located on the wrong side of the socioeconomic tracks," Jen said. "That's where I met my husband, Jeffrey, who worked for Youth for Christ." She admits that part of her motivation for marrying Jeff was her hope that she could "ride on his coattails."

"His ministry coattails?" I asked.

"Yes, at that time both my husband and I believed that women could do anything *except* be a senior pastor."

Jen and Jeffrey spent the next ten years serving as youth pastors in a variety of churches. Eventually Jeff gave up the ministry and went to work for Microsoft. Soon after, they began attending a megachurch. Young people in particular flock to this church, seeking an uncompromised set of instructions on the right way to live. When Jen and her husband began attending, the church had just moved to a new campus.

"This was the first church I attended that had groups for women who had suffered from sexual abuse, so I joined," says Jen. "After hearing my predatory youth pastor story, the woman who was leading the group talked with the pastor. He searched the Internet and discovered that my former youth pastor/abuser was still doing youth ministry just a few hours away from us. My pastor and another staff member drove down and confronted the man, who confessed to them. I felt protected and validated; it was an amazing experience." However, Jen was about to discover once again that when it comes to church, protection often comes at a price.

Jen is a thinker. She's intellectually curious and likes to learn. During this time she went back to school and completed her undergraduate studies, earning a BA in psychology. Her church was an early adopter of using the Internet as a means of communicating with its members, and Jen enjoyed engaging in her church's members-only online forum. She and her pastor would sometimes go head-to-head on theological issues. This seemed to frustrate her pastor, who would periodically comment to the men, "Why do I have to have this discussion with a woman? Come on, you guys." The pastor was clear about his belief that women are designed primarily to be helpmates to their husbands. He challenged the men in his church to "man up" and learn doctrine so they could teach their wives at home.

"One time in the online forum I suggested that Christian men and women could have nonromantic chaste friendships," Jen says. "That led to a spirited discussion. I didn't realize that my pastor was tracking the conversation. He came out to say he vehemently disagreed with my views and chose to express his outrage at my ideas *in writing on the forum.* In a message addressed to my husband (who wasn't participating in the forum), the pastor told him that he needed to convince me to shut up."

For Jen, protection from another form of abuse came with a price tag . . . submission and silence.

"Needless to say, that was the end of our time at that church," Jen says.

Jen refused to quit Jesus, however.

In spite of a hundred legitimate reasons to walk away, Jen was about to go *all in* on her Jesus bet and *re-sign.*

Todd Hunter came to speak at the seminary Jen was attending in Seattle. He was looking for men *and women* who were interested in planting churches on the West Coast.

"I wasn't able to make the meeting, but another student told me about Todd. I'd heard about the denomination he's part of a few years earlier through another friend in Chicago and liked what I heard. It sounded so different, and I was pretty much done with the low-church evangelicalism I had grown up with. That system taught me that the way to solve my problems was to pray more, read the Bible more, be involved in more church programs, and go to Christian counseling. I had done all of those things yet was still bleeding profusely.

"What I found in the sacramental theology was the reality of 'Christ in you, the hope of glory.' While not providing any kind of magic cure for my wounding, it did provide an alternate way of understanding Christ's presence that cognitive-based Christian counseling didn't." Jen was particularly attuned to counseling because she was in seminary pursuing a degree in counseling.

Things changed for her when one day in class her professor said, "I know this is a class for everyone—both counseling students and MDiv students—and that most of you are counseling students. But I think some of you who are pursuing a counseling degree in hopes of helping individuals—and in so doing finding healing for yourself—might be more likely to find the healing you're pursuing by leading an entire faith community." And with that the desire to lead a spiritual community that had been dormant in Jennifer's heart sprang to life. Following a period of discerning what direction she needed to go, she switched to the MDiv program.

"I sought Todd out, and when we talked my first two questions were, Are you willing to support women pastors? And can someone like me, who isn't the typical church-planting type, be successful at this? He answered yes to both, and we were off."

Given Jennifer's negative track record with male Christian leaders, I was curious about what had changed for her. What gave her the will to try again with yet another male leader? Why didn't she just walk away like several of the other women I interviewed had?

She told me about Jeff and Dan.

"Let me tell you about my husband, Jeff. No one predicted success for our marriage. We met and got engaged in under a month. My sexual abuse, which lasted into my late teens, had ended only five years earlier, and I was seriously floundering on my own without any emotional support from the church or my family. Our first year was miserable—we fought and were completely unreasonable with each other. We had no idea how to sustain a deep friendship, never mind a marriage. We both had big aspirations for ministry, but little education and even less financial support."

Then came a turning point. "In our second year of marriage, Jeff was offered a ministry job across the country. We left our home in California in a U-Haul truck and trailer, towing our car and heading east. The morning of the second day, we left the hotel in Nevada where we had spent the night and traveled an hour down the road, where we stopped for gas. But somehow when we were pulling into the gas station, we managed to squeeze around a tight corner in such a way that the U-Haul and trailer were caught on either side of a pole. We tried for over an hour to get the truck unstuck, but that only made things worse. We were so frustrated. We stood outside the U-Haul and tried to talk to truckers as they walked past. We begged for advice and even offered to pay them to get us unstuck. But no one could help.

"During this ordeal, all of the immature interpersonal dynamics that had been playing out in our first year of marriage were in full swing. We were stuck in the middle of the desert at a gas station, as frustrated as we could be, and no one was able to help us. We did the only thing we could. We figured out how to unload our car from the trailer. Then we unlatched the trailer from the truck. After moving the truck, we rehitched and loaded the trailer. Even though we'd only traveled sixty miles that day, we were exhausted, dehydrated, and emotionally spent. We were done. We found the nearest hotel, checked in, and hid from the world for the rest of the day.

"I don't remember us having an epiphany about how great it was that when we were up against a wall, we could work together to get ourselves out of a jam. Mostly I remember napping, watching TV, and ordering delivery pizza. But eventually, as we drove east and had time to reflect on the experience, it became a metaphor for us—a kind of shorthand for the fact that even though we longed to be embraced by a larger community, *all we really had was each other*. And from there we grew in our understanding of how to support each other and how to receive support. We still talk fondly about this incident today because it was the metaphor for a change we needed."

Sixteen years later, Jen calls her husband her biggest supporter. "Jeff's support is the reason I was able to go back to school. Whenever I talk about a dream I have for ministry, he is always trying to get me to see an even more beautiful vision. His belief that I can accomplish these dreams has given me the courage to try."

By the time she and Jeff had been married for seven years, their relationship was strong. They had a two-year-old son, and Jen was working full time at a good church. From the outside, her life appeared stable.

But on a deeper level, Jen says, she was in spiritual crisis, and even though she was working for a church, she no longer felt any connection to God, even though she wanted to. Then she met another person who helped restore her faith. Like Jen, Dan Brennan participated in an online e-mail list to discuss subjects related to theology and culture. Dan befriended Jen and asked her questions to better understand the disconnect she was feeling and how her early life might have contributed to it. He suggested some books that might help her, and they began to pray together on the phone every week.

"The experience of having another person listen to my grief without being frightened off by the enormity of my need was very healing—and then to have that person help me pray through those things was life changing," Jen says.

"One thing I desperately needed to learn, although I was not even aware of this need before I met Dan, was that I could be loved by a man and be in a close relationship with him without it being sexual. As odd as it may sound, I sometimes failed to truly believe and receive my husband's love because, since we had a sexual relationship, at some level I wondered if he was just being political to get what he wanted. Or I would think of my sexual abuse, which came from the only man who mattered in my life during my teenage decade, and would feel that because my husband couldn't love me without needing sexual contact with me, then no one could. He was pastor to me after all.

"But Dan was a man who was willing to love me and walk with me when things were messy, who got nothing sexual out of the arrangement. This was incredibly healing for me. Through this I have learned to trust other men. Frankly, I'm not sure I would have been able to trust Todd without having had this experience.

"Over the years, people have expressed anxiety about the possibility of a chaste nonromantic friendship between a man and a woman. Interestingly enough, our spouses have never done so—they have both been deep supporters of our friendship. Dan's wife has blessed me many times by praying beautiful prayers about my friendship with her husband, and Jeff has deeply encouraged me by the trust he places in me as his faithful wife.

"Dan's book *Sacred Unions, Sacred Passions* is his theological reflection on a number of friendships that he has had with women. I suspect many women could use a male friend like Dan, who would honor and encourage them to become whatever God has made them to be," Jen adds.

• • •

My Take

Jennifer's story made me think about all the women Jesus interacted with. The Samaritan woman. The woman who begged for the crumbs off the table. The woman caught in the act of adultery. The woman (his mother) who asked him to turn the water into wine. The woman who prostrated herself at his feet, kissed them numerous times, washed them with her tears, and let her hair down to dry them. The sisters of Lazarus, Martha and Mary. The women who stood by him when he was crucified while most of the men hid. The woman Jesus met privately in a garden, who was the first person he chose to appear to following his resurrection.

As I've said, while it's true that Jesus didn't have favorites, he did play favorites. He was soft on outsiders and hard on insiders. His favorite group of outsiders seemed to be women. Jesus delighted in aligning with them, honoring them, and elevating them.

Jen has been healed from the hurt one man inflicted on her by three important men: her husband, her friend, and her bishop. Together these three men have become the voice, hands, feet, and ears of Jesus. Through them he has aligned with, honored, and elevated Jen, who is now on her way to being ordained as a priest and becoming one of the first female church planters in her denomination.

Fast Facts

72% say **I possess a lot of spiritual freedom in my life.**

Our Bloggers Said

Several years ago I walked away from the church (not God, but the church). This is where I found freedom, freedom to become who I was called to be. Outside of the church is where I could hear His voice and His calling on my life, away from the institution that was telling me what a good Christian woman should be doing.

■ ■ ■

I have happily put any ministry or career aspirations on hold to raise my precious babies (preschool and toddler age). . . . Not only do I not resent my wife and mother role now, but I love every minute of it and believe this is the most rewarding job and exactly what I was created to do!

■ ■ ■

My husband and I have been involved in a progressive, nontraditional church for almost three years now. Part of my deprogramming process was seeing that I was, in fact, capable of leadership in the church (beyond the kitchen committee), and my opinions were as valuable as my husband's concerning spiritual things. It has certainly been a Damascus road experience . . . *grace* . . . and freedom in Christ.

CHAPTER 18

THE BLUE DOT BLOGGERS

Keep It Real, but Keep It to Yourself

IT'S DIFFICULT TO ADMIT, but in general the church is not a safe place to be yourself. That became evident to me as I was writing this book. I received numerous e-mails, Facebook messages, and blog post comments from women and even a few men. They heard I was looking for stories. Many of the women requested that I hide their identities lest their jobs, church roles, or marriages be threatened. That's why this chapter is called "The Blue Dot Bloggers." I'm not revealing their names.

In the end, my biggest challenge wasn't finding stories but choosing stories. I was overwhelmed by the number of women who were eager to talk about their experiences. You've read some of the comments on the Fast Facts pages. Because I think the input I received online provides some nuance I may not have captured in the main interviews, I decided to create one chapter using some of the feedback I didn't have time to develop more fully. I've added headings; otherwise, only the spelling and punctuation have been cleaned up when necessary to make the blog postings easier to read. *Warning:* As you read, prepare to feel uncomfortable at times.

Eve's Treachery Ran in My Blood

The church I grew up in was a safe place. The senior pastor and his wife were like grandparents. The church was my home. Even though my church loved me, it wounded me as well. My soul felt battered with the certainty that God would have loved me more if I'd been a man. He would have trusted me more, valued me more.

In my church, women were not pastors or elders. Our place was in our homes, serving our husbands, letting them lead. They told me it was because I was more easily deceived, that Eve's treachery ran in my blood. I tried my best to meet their expectations, but in so many ways I failed. I was strong where I should have been meek; I spoke where they expected silence. I was creative instead of domestic. Not really a leader, but not a good follower either.

Naively, I thought my church would be home forever. But things change. We were growing apart, only I didn't know it. I came across books that showed me that what I had been taught about myself, about women, about God, was wrong. As I read, prayed, and cried, the truth sank deep into that bleeding, scarred place in my soul.

The pain I could not even identify began to fade. My confidence grew, my creativity exploded, and my husband seemed to prefer that over another dependent clinging to him. At church we were told that women were not inferior to men. Oh no—*just different*. We didn't need power. We had "influence." My husband and I left.

Now I feel as though the entire world is mine, to hold and love and serve. God's passion for me—for the woman I am—shakes me to the foundations of my soul and makes me long to pour it out on others. I am flawed, but he loves me anyway. In that love, I'm strong, powerful, beautiful, and whole. I am home.

Is This What They Meant by Sex Education?

In the evangelical churches I attended growing up, traditional gender roles were portrayed, taught, and even encouraged from elementary age up. Girls did one activity; boys did another. Our teachers pointed to the actions of women in Bible stories as fodder for what "godly" women do. In youth group, boys and girls took on different roles: at events, girls prepared, served food, and cleaned up. Boys set up the sound systems, chairs, and electronics. Girls were complimented for having "humility" and "a servant's heart," and boys were encouraged to be leaders.

In an issue all its own, we were taught that male sexuality is an almost-uncontrollable force that must not be tempted. Women must "avoid tempting the boys," and in the name of modesty, take responsibility for the eyes and libidos of their male counterparts.

I never remember a pastor talking to the boys and young men about self-control and respect for women. It was always a warning not to be "tempted by women." I do remember hearing middle-aged female youth volunteers or pastors' wives (we never had women pastors) warn the girls not to tempt the boys, not to dress inappropriately. "Those are your brothers, and you need *to protect their eyes.*"

Islam has a saying about women having "nine parts of desire." When Allah created women and men, he gave nine parts of desire to the woman, and one part to the man. So women must be covered and separated because their sexuality is dangerous. That is effectively the very same thing I witnessed in twenty-six years in the evangelical church.

What's with Men and Coffee?

I used to work at a Christian college, and my program shared space with an MDiv program for pastors. A few of them asked me to get them coffee on more than one occasion. I would smile nicely and tell them to help themselves as I pointed in the direction of the kitchen. And forget about anyone but the two women who worked there making more when it ran out—even though it took about a minute and a half to get a new pot going. I just don't understand why so many men seem incapable of making coffee. It's just not that hard.

I Tried Everything

I was raised in a legalistic, Bible-teaching church. If a woman had a question during an open forum, she was to give the question to her husband, father, or some other man to ask for her. Men were the heads of the household. Women were not allowed to manage money beyond that necessary for buying groceries and running errands. Women were not encouraged to go to college, since it was not biblical for them to work outside the home (especially mothers).

I feared God and the consequences of not being obedient. But I also wanted to go to college. My father was an academic. Learning was valued in my family. So I attended a women's college on the East Coast. Despite the fact that I was more conservative than many of my friends, I felt accepted for who I was, and as a multiracial woman, I fit in better there than I ever had in my mostly white Midwestern community at home.

But I wasn't ready for a total departure from my conservative comfort zone. The summer after my freshman year, I began dating a man back home. We got engaged, I graduated, and we married. I did work for the first couple of years of our marriage. None of our friends said much about it—after all, we didn't have children yet.

Our marriage was not good, even from the beginning. My husband was prone to lying and often unkind. He was brooding, and I was on edge. Sometimes he called me names. He often ignored me. I was advised to "love more," "cook dinners," and "submit more." Unfortunately none of those things seemed to do anything to bolster his integrity or leadership.

Church friends asked me repeatedly when we were going to have children, but I was disappointed by the instability of my marriage, by the lies, by the questionable behavior, and by the lack of partnership that I craved. I felt insecure and alone.

I was confused by my desire to learn about theology and the fact that teaching seemed to be in my spiritual gifting. A woman was not to teach a man, but I had never enjoyed working with children despite teaching Sunday school at the encouragement of others. I did not enjoy women's Bible studies on Wednesday mornings either. My concerns about my marriage, when I shared them, were met with platitudes.

I was deeply lonely, but I was berated by those close to me for being "high maintenance." After all, I had a good-looking husband who made a lot of money (despite the fact that I was never allowed to know where it was, let alone be a part of major financial decisions), a big home, and a nice car. No one heard the things he said behind closed doors or knew what my life was really like. It would take years before I would come to recognize my husband's emotional abuse. I suspected him of having affairs, but my questions were met with denial, lies, and insults. I began to dream of a life on my own, but I knew I could never leave without biblical grounds, which boiled down to adultery or abandonment.

I did try to be more submissive, more assertive, and more mysterious. I tried to woo him. I tried to befriend him. I tried to speak my mind. I tried everything.

For the next decade, I went in and out of depression. I combed the Scriptures and their contexts. I searched for answers. I wondered why I wanted more out of life than just to live in unquestioning silence. I didn't understand why I had more leadership qualities than my husband and was more interested in matters of God. None of my efforts or my submission had produced the results they were supposed to.

I was slowly dying. My family, who had become more liberal in their theology of marriage and divorce, were deeply concerned about me. One day, I decided that God's grace was either enough for me or it wasn't. That my decision to stay or not in this marriage was not going to determine my salvation. That God knew my heart and how much I had wanted to do what was right—no matter how difficult or painful.

Realizing that I might need to support myself someday, I went back to work. I had not worked in a decade. I did not have any retirement funds. I was deeply afraid about my choices and decisions and the future. I also prepared for the possibility that if I left I might be disciplined by the church and lose the majority of my church friends.

Strangely, my marriage improved. For a few years, it

seemed to be the best it had ever been. Perhaps it was that we both had our space and time alone—my job involved regular travel. My husband enjoyed his autonomy. I gained some self-esteem. We even considered starting a family.

However, I eventually discovered my husband was having an affair with a stripper he met on a trip. Even after his confession, he would not make a choice between his mistress and me. I waited to see what he would do. My husband would not give her up. Eventually, I filed for divorce.

My husband had a child with his mistress and married her after our divorce was final. I have never been disappointed in God. But I remained deeply hurt by and disappointed in the church for years.

I have changed much of my theology about the place of women in the church and in marriage. Today I teach through my writing. And I'm delivering my first church sermon in a few months. I have never had children and am skittish about the thought of remarriage.

Happy at Home

I'm not lying or deceived when I say the traditional women's roles bring me great joy and satisfaction. I think that in general, God made us that way. I mean, our bodies are made to conceive, grow, carry, and feed the children; doesn't it just make sense then that God also made us better equipped to take care of them? And what's more glorious and important than raising children and seeing them become good, happy, and healthy adults? It might not get as much fame, but it's a lot more valuable if you ask me! Plus, I hear a lot of women say they work because staying home is too hard. So who's really escaping reality? Well, I won't be your judge; go to God and ask him to reveal your motives.

Anyone Can't—A Twentysomething Woman's Thoughtful Analysis

I think evangelical women, in general, are under tremendous pressure to appear happy. We receive messages from every corner that truly godly women are happy and content with their lot in life. "God is good all the time!" . . . What woman . . . wants to be heard complaining about her church? It's just not becoming to a "woman of faith."

I think there's also a general aversion to appearing "feminist" (however they understand it) among evangelical women. In many ways, feminism has lost among evangelicals because so many women who value family, children, and other "traditional" things feel threatened by aspects of the secular feminist agenda.

I wonder how many women actually know what their pastor, elders, or church leaders believe about women's roles. I wonder how many of them know the real limitations that are present in their congregations. Most of the time, especially in contemporary evangelical churches, these limitations are unspoken and remain so until challenged.

For example, a friend of mine visited a nondenominational

"community of house churches" in our area. She asked one of the pastors who in the church could be an elder. His initial response was, "Anyone." But she pressed the matter further and said, "So, as a single woman, I could be an elder?" His response was, "Well, no. If you were a married woman, you and your husband could be elders. But not single women." And she replied, "So, anyone can't be an elder." He said, "Uh, yeah. I guess not."

Hierarchy Is Holy

I fail to see how anyone *cannot* see hierarchy in the Trinity. Jesus deferred to his Father. He "sent" the Spirit. Is there some kind of belief that hierarchy determines value and (in) equality? . . .

The three persons of the Trinity, being God, *are decidedly male* in expression. There is no gender issue. Thus the idea that hierarchy is somehow inherently a bad thing must extend into all realms of redeemed life: church polity; the workplace; who calls the shots in emergency situations. The idea that hierarchy itself is an evil thing doesn't hold water.

Hierarchy Is Heresy

Outside of cultural mutations, the Orthodox position of the church has affirmed the equality of all persons of the Trinity. . . . *The Trinity was co-opted by misogynists*, and the Son and Spirit subordinated to the Father to counter modern American cultural trends toward egalitarianism.

Sometimes the oppressed choose to settle for "better" or "good enough" instead of fighting to stop their oppression altogether. I don't say that lightly or without sensitivity—I've never experienced oppression. I can't imagine how exhausting it would be, and how tempting the option of "good enough" might be.

CHAPTER 19

PRESIDENT, SURE!
PASTOR, SHHH!

THE 2008 PRESIDENTIAL ELECTION featured two women, Hillary Clinton and Sarah Palin. They were miles apart politically, but joined at the hip historically.

For the first time, two women competed for one of the nation's two highest offices. Had it not been for another historic first—an African American on the ballot—odds are that one of them would be president or vice president today.

Once again, however, history told women to get in line.

Interestingly, both women claim Christianity as their religion of choice. But Sarah Palin's church forbids women from being elders or preaching on Sundays.[1] On the other hand, Hillary Clinton's mainline denomination has been ordaining women for fifty years. However, very few female pastors make it to the top. Most serve in one of two places—the academy (a university such as Duke) or a small rural church.[2]

Here's what I find ironic: while Clinton and Palin both have a fair shot at being elected the leader of the free world (by a lot of cheering men, no doubt), neither of them could or would stand much of a chance being chosen senior pastor of their own churches.

If the church weren't as profoundly dependent on women as it is, this would be less of an issue. But clearly if women walked out the door, the church would be in grave trouble. When George Barna calls women "the backbone of activity in the typical conventional church,"[3] he offers these numbers to back up his statement:

- A majority of weekly churchgoers (53 percent) are women.
- Small groups that meet for prayer or Bible study are made up primarily of women (60 percent).
- Sunday school programs for adults are also more likely to be attended by women (59 percent).
- The majority of church volunteers (57 percent) are females.[4]

David Kinnaman, president of The Barna Group, makes an even more startling claim: "The typical profile of an involved Christian is a married woman in her early fifties."[5]

In other words, if an alien from outer space landed in North America and asked to be introduced to the typical Christian, it would soon find itself talking with a woman.

Yet in spite of the centrality of women in the church and the fact that without them the local church would probably cease to function, only 10 percent of the senior pastors of Protestant churches in America are women.[6] That's true even though "women in the pulpit are generally more highly educated than their male counterparts. Currently, more than three-quarters of female pastors (77%) have a seminary degree. Among male pastors less than two-thirds (63%) can make that same claim."[7]

If the church were a democracy, this would be called taxation without representation. If it were an ethnic issue, it would be called discrimination. If it were a power issue, it would be called sexism.

I began the book by explaining why this issue is personal for me and why, I believe, it directly affects you, too. Then I told you the stories of women who have had to face this issue in one way or another. In the final two chapters, I invite you to step back with me and consider how women's influence is expanding within the wider culture and, finally, how they might experience increasing influence in the church as well.

Moving On Up: Women on the Job

In 2010, women made up the majority of the workforce in the United States for the first time in the nation's history—a testimony to the profound influence women are already making outside the church culture. In an *Atlantic* article examining this milestone, Hanna Rosin pointed out other indicators that women are playing an increasingly important role in the labor force:

Women dominate the fastest-growing employment sectors. Of the fifteen job categories projected to grow the most in the next decade, all but two are occupied primarily by women.[8]

The majority of middle managers are women. Women are beginning to dominate middle management and professional careers. The Bureau of Labor Statistics reports that women hold 51.4 percent of managerial and professional jobs—up from 26.1 percent in 1980. Fifty-four percent of all accountants are female, as are about half of those employed in banking and insurance. About a third of America's physicians, as well as 45 percent of associates in law firms, are women.[9]

Nevertheless, 97 percent of CEOs in major international corporations are men. Despite the abundance of women in lower-level positions, very few women make it to the top. Rosin writes that "prominent female CEOs, past and present, are so rare that they count as minor celebrities . . . only 3 percent of Fortune 500 CEOs are women, and the number has never risen much above that."[10]

Rosin and other writers also explain why some men are uncomfortable with women's growing influence.

Female chief executives earn more than their male counterparts. Female CEOs may still be underrepresented in America's largest companies; but as Rosin points out, "They are highly prized: last year, they outearned their male counterparts by 43 percent, on average, and received bigger raises. . . . The association is clear: innovative, successful firms are the ones that promote women."[11]

Women start about 50 percent of all new businesses. In spite of this fact, less than 7 percent of the start-ups funded by venture capital firms in the past decade are headed by women.[12]

Women would probably make more money than men if funded properly. A Babson College study projected that if female entrepreneurs began with the same capital as their male counterparts, they would add six million jobs to the economy in five years, including two million in the first year.[13]

Then There's Hollywood

While most of corporate America is closing the gender gap, there is one place that surprisingly remains stuck in the past—Hollywood! If you compare the church with the movie industry, it's a virtual draw as to which one of them allows women *the least* amount of influence. Both systems appear to be quite comfortable using women's bodies (albeit for very different purposes) but not their brains.

Producers and directors are the power brokers in Hollywood. And based on the industry's awards, it would appear that women show little interest in producing or directing. The facts, however, show otherwise. Women have been directing films for decades, but Hollywood has refused to reward them the success they have earned. In fact, it appears that the system has thrown up blockades to impede them.

In 2010 Kathryn Bigelow won the Best Director Oscar for *The Hurt Locker*. This was the first time a woman won the Oscar for directing. In the eighty-one years before that, only three women had even been *nominated* for an Oscar for direction.

Martha Lauzen, executive director for the Center for the Study of Women in Television and Film at San Diego State University, reports that "women accounted for 7 percent of directors in 2009, a decrease of 2 percentage points from 2008. This figure represents no change from the percentage of women directing in 1987."[14]

I couldn't help but notice that the percentage of women Hollywood *rewards* for using their brains correlates closely with the percentage of women the church *allows* to be senior pastors. When you see these same patterns in diverse systems, it makes one wonder if what we're dealing with isn't a gender issue at all. Maybe it's more primal than that. Maybe it's a power struggle. Those who have it (men) don't want to give it up to those who lack it (women).

Power at Play

Statistics are helpful, but stories are better. Here's how this power struggle played out recently in a small mainline church in the rural Midwest. This church is part of one of the most theologically, liberal denominations in the United States (although you might get its members confused with fundamentalists after reading this story).

A female churchgoer, let's call her Karina, lives in a small Ohio town with her husband, who farms soybeans, corn, and wheat. The couple has attended the same church for over thirty years. A number of years ago, when the church's pastor took a new assignment, the area bishop assigned a new pastor—a woman. Since their denomination has been ordaining women pastors for decades, the members of this church knew about and ostensibly agreed with this practice. But they'd never actually had a woman pastor before. This was their maiden voyage, and it got stormy very quickly.

During the last two years of the woman pastor's seven-year term, Karina served as chairperson of the pastor-parish committee. This gave her a front-row seat for the soap opera I call *When Men Aren't Happy at Church*. You might confuse this list of harassments with a screenplay for a bad movie.

Here's what this woman pastor experienced, as seen from Karina's perspective:

Before she came, we had an active youth group
with a part-time youth worker/pastor; we had had a

part-time youth worker for approximately eighteen to twenty years. Coincidentally the existing youth worker left just prior to the new pastor's arrival, and she was told there would be no replacement hired and she would need to do the job. At the time, there were probably twenty youth meeting regularly. During her tenure that number increased to about forty-five. (This in a small-town church of two hundred.)

Even though she had a budget for travel, books/materials, continuing education, etc., she had to ask permission prior to spending any of it. The trustees would carefully scrutinize and often veto her use of funds, even though the use was completely normal and acceptable. Additionally, she had to prepare and submit detailed records of how she spent her time, and when that time routinely added up to 60–70 hours a week, she was accused of padding her records. No other pastor had been subjected to this level of scrutiny in the past.

As a pastor, there were complaints that her planning skills and her communications skills were inadequate when working with adults. She was fine when working with children and youth because that is usually a woman's strong point, but not adults. I evaluated her planning and communication skills as above average at all levels, which I based on a comparison of those with whom I work every day in a business setting.

Perhaps her most serious infraction was that when the trustees would attempt to tell her that the congregation should not participate in a church growth program or allow Narcotics Anonymous to meet in one of the rooms, she would "defy" them by reminding them what denominational polity said concerning the bounds of their authority and then do it.

But the very last straw that convinced the bishop to pull her from our church was the petition that was sent by approximately thirty husbands *and their wives*. They made sure that it bypassed me, the pastor, and the district superintendent (all women) so that the complaints could be heard directly by the bishop. The complaint was specifically that our pastor did not have the skills necessary to shepherd adults, though she was fine with children. They also included a quote from the Bible as evidence that women should not be in charge of men. Even though they'd been part of a denomination that had been ordaining women for fifty years.

All of this bad behavior disturbed Karina, and she eventually left this church. The truth of how the congregation treated their pastor, and by association Karina, led her to reexamine the role this supposed Christian community played in her life. Currently Karina is in the process of exploring how Christian community can be found outside the traditional walls. She has experienced God's presence in working with women in recovery from substance and alcohol abuse at a transitional house and in occasionally worshiping with a campus community at a local Catholic college. She is still searching for a congregation in her rural area that openly welcomes women at all levels of worship and leadership.

Let's Go to Hollywood Again

One of the largest Pentecostal denominations in the world grew out of a church founded by a woman. Aimee Semple McPherson launched the Angelus Temple, which ended up spawning off the International Church of the Foursquare Gospel.

Sister Aimee was something of a showwoman. She loved spectacle and built a church that fit perfectly in the Hollywood scene.[15] She purchased property near Echo Park and dedicated Angelus Temple on January 1, 1923. By the time she was thirty-three years old, Aimee Semple McPherson had established the first Christian radio station in the United States, a 5,300-seat auditorium in which thousands of people were saved and healed, a Bible college, and ultimately a denomination, all of which are still in operation today. The International Church of the Foursquare Gospel now has well over 1.9 million members, with over 31,000 churches and meeting places in seventy-two countries around the world.

Notice how men began taking over what a woman started:

- By 1944, the year McPherson died, women accounted for 67 percent of the ordained clergy in the denomination.
- By 1979, the figure had dropped to 42 percent.
- By 1993, the number of ordained women had decreased to approximately 38 percent.[16]
- Today, of the 6,000 credentialed ministers in the Foursquare Church, only about 151 are female senior pastors.[17]

Unlike many conservative denominations that seem to hide their policy on women, the Foursquare Church is quite open about its official policy regarding women in ministry: "Anyone called by God and verified through character, spiritual experience and preparation for service or leadership is qualified for Foursquare Church ministry in any role or office, regardless of gender, age or ethnicity."[18]

So I asked a young female pastor who is on staff in a large Foursquare church on the West Coast if her experience matched up with this statement. She said this:

I went to seminary because I felt like it would help give weight to my voice as a woman. I care deeply about helping women see themselves as equals. They battle against it in pop culture and at work. The last place they should experience a feeling of being "lesser than" is at church. I want to change that from the inside. But here's what's discouraging. In my home church we've only had two female speakers in the past twelve years. I asked my pastor, why? His response, "It's just not something our church is comfortable with." Here's what I think—I think it's just not something he's comfortable with.

The Foursquare Gospel church would be wise to pay close attention to this thirtysomething woman pastor because according to a Barna report issued in 2000, the median age of women who attend, volunteer in, and give money to churches is somewhere between fifty-six and fifty-nine years old.[19] That's called a dying breed. They need all the help my young friend is willing to give if they hope to lower that median age.[20]

How the World's Largest Church Got That Way

Most church leaders want a bigger church. But where did the idea of the megachurch originate? Who developed the concept? When seeking answers, one place you will inevitably end up is the front steps of the Yoido Full Gospel Church in Seoul, Korea, founded and led by Pastor David Yonggi Cho. With over 200,000 in attendance, this is the largest congregation in the world.[21]

Two things fascinate me about the world's largest church:

1. How utterly dependent it was upon women for its success.
2. How few churches follow its example.

Women have always played a central role in Pastor Cho's spiritual life and church success.

Cho converted to Christianity at the age of nineteen, after an unknown girl visited him daily to tell him about Jesus Christ after he had been diagnosed with terminal tuberculosis. One day, she knelt down to pray for him and began to weep. He was deeply touched and told her, "Don't cry. I now know about your Christian love. Since I am dying I will become a Christian for you." She gave him her own Bible and said to him, "If you read it faithfully, you will find the words of life." He recovered from his illness, and in 1956 he received a scholarship to study theology at Full Gospel Bible College in Seoul. While there, he met his future mother-in-law, who also became his close ministerial associate.[22]

Given the number of church growth seminars pastors attend and their desire to bring more people into their churches, it's no surprise that churches have tried everything from smoke machines to ten-piece rock bands and light shows to draw more people. While all of these practices apparently pass Jesus' theological test, when it comes to giving women the green light to lead, it seems most churches need a committee to even consider that question.

If history is any indicator, churches grow numerically

when women are given the opportunity to lead without restriction, particularly when they form an authentic, respectful partnership with men—at least that's how the world's largest church got to where it is today. Here's what Pastor Cho had to say about the critical role women played in his success.

In 1964 [when Cho was very ill] I had the choice of one of two steps—to delegate my ministry to lay Christians or keep up the ministry. But when I tried to delegate my ministry to the men, they would all make excuses saying that they were too busy, or not trained, or "You receive a salary not me."

So I had to use women. In Korean society—for long periods of time—women had no power or voice in the church, and I began to use women. This was a big risk—but I had no choice—it was a step out in faith, and I had no alternative. Then the women made a tremendous contribution to church growth! Now all the Korean churches—even Catholic—have accepted women. When I come to Europe and America encouraging pastors to use women, I always receive a lot of opposition—especially in Europe.

Secondly, I want to stress the importance of the use of women. Women are underused in the church. So women are a tremendous strength in church because of culture—but in Western culture—you are afraid of using women. But once women were given the freedom to work as fellow leaders there was an explosion of Cell Leaders."[23]

Here are the numbers at Yoida Full Gospel Church:

- 50,000 cell groups, 47,000 (94 percent) led by women.
- 600 associate pastors, 400 (67 percent) are women.[24]

American Christians have a tendency to dismiss these kinds of statistics from foreign churches. We do so at our own peril.

While Cho was using women to advance the Kingdom of God, South Korean culture was also making some major changes regarding how they treated women. In her compelling article "The End of Men," Hanna Rosin notes,

Over several centuries, South Korea, for instance, constructed one of the most rigid patriarchal societies in the world. Many wives who failed to produce male heirs were abused and treated as domestic servants. . . . Then, in the 1970s and '80s, the government embraced an industrial revolution and encouraged women to enter the labor force. Women moved to the city and went to college. They advanced rapidly, from industrial jobs to clerical jobs to professional work. The traditional order began to crumble soon after.[25]

What Rosin doesn't acknowledge is that, while this massive shift was occurring, Cho's church was growing rapidly and becoming a tour de force in South Korea. Furthermore, Cho located his church in the middle of Seoul, the destination of many women wanting to find promising jobs. It's fascinating to consider that Cho's courage to use women in his church may have helped ignite a cultural revolution for women in his country. Was it Cho's willingness to give women visibility, authority, and opportunity that enabled the South Korean government to observe a large enough social sample to see the benefit of treating women as equals? We don't know, but the sociological data is compelling.

What if the church of Jesus followed Pastor Cho's example and stopped conforming itself to the world's way of treating women? What if it no longer linked itself either with conservatives or liberals and instead followed in the footsteps of our master, the Lord Jesus, who went out of his way to honor, elevate, and create equality for women wherever he went?

Has the Jesus Revolution Reached Your Heart?

In his provocative book *Sacred Unions, Sacred Passions*, Dan Brennan goes where very few Christian men have dared to go. Dan takes another look at John 20 and suggests that Jesus' choice to reveal himself first to a woman following his resurrection was intentionally designed to make a statement. As he says,

Jesus' choice to reveal his resurrected self to Mary [Magdalene], before meeting Peter, before . . . John, and before . . . other male and female followers puts male-female friendship right at the center of Christianity's pivotal moment. This opens up the possibility for an entirely different script for male-female friendship within the new creation that God has birthed in Christ.[26]

Given the frequency with which Jesus interacted with women . . .

Given the honor he consistently extended toward them . . .

Given the questionable circumstances in which he allowed himself to be seen with women . . .

Given the radical departure and risks he took to elevate women within his religious culture . . .

It's not hard to imagine that if Jesus were transported into American culture today and behaved accordingly, he undoubtedly would be accused of being a radical feminist by the religionists of our day.

Catherine Mowry LaCugna describes the revolutionary way Jesus behaved toward women: "Contrary to the conventions of his day, Jesus was not afraid to speak with or touch women, even when he was alone with them and there was the greatest possibility for creating scandal and discrediting his ministry."[27]

This Jesus revolution lifts the conversation above simplistic conservative or liberal divides and challenges our hearts on the deepest level. It confronts our fears and assumptions. It is truly a new way of living.

Like the vast majority of male Christians, most female Christians have no desire to lead or become senior pastors.

What many of them do want is the same opportunities men have to respond to the gifts and callings of God wherever they lead.

They want a world where Hillary or Sarah could be elected president *and* a church where they or their daughters, sisters, or mothers could be elected pastor.

CHAPTER 20

WHEN ONLY A WOMAN WILL DO

OUR COUNTRY HAS NEVER BEEN MORE DIVIDED THAN IT IS TODAY. I believe we are still fighting a "civil war," only this time it's being waged online. We blog-cheer for our cable news celebrities and blog-jeer the other teams. We've become expert at comparing *our* best with *others'* worst. This same spirit carries over into the conversation about women in the church.

After talking with many thoughtful Christian men and women, I can report unequivocally that when it comes to how we think about women in the church, Christians are deeply and profoundly divided. What's particularly confusing to the Outsiders who are watching us is that both sides use the same Bible passages to come to two completely different sets of conclusions.

As the stories in this book show, the question about women's roles in the church also elicits a wide range of opinions from women themselves. Given this divide—and all the other challenges facing pastors and church leaders—it's tempting to consider doing nothing about helping women gain more influence. If you are a follower of Jesus, however, that is simply an unacceptable option.

I hope the stories in this book have helped you to see that a number of women—particularly younger women—are either moving away or staying away from the church because the message they're hearing is that their gifts and leadership skills are not valued there—that is, unless they want to serve in children's or women's ministries. This not only negatively affects these women, it also hurts the church. After researching the relationships between men and women in the workplace (including the church), Shaunti Feldhahn commented on the impact of keeping women out of leadership in the local church:

> The most important problem involves the impact on the mission of the church. Without at all intending it and with the best of intentions, many churches by lacking female perspective in leadership may be limiting the effectiveness or reach of the work God intends for them to do.

Feldhahn, who is no feminist, admits,

This subject is hard to navigate because it is so tied
up with the debate over whether the Bible reserves
the solo pulpit role for men when teaching the whole
church, or whether that was a cultural caution that
should not be "law" today. . . . Believers with good
intentions are trying to follow scriptural mandates
on how men and women relate but perhaps in some
cases going beyond Scripture or don't realize that
how they are applying Scripture leads to an end
result that seems unlikely to be what God intended.[1]

Feldhahn is more polite than I. Here is the problem in a
nutshell as I see it:

Christians who believe men and women have equal influence in the church have a pre-Fall paradigm, meaning men and
women equally express the image of God. For them, gifts, not
gender, determine who does what in the Kingdom. Those who
hold a post-Fall paradigm believe that Eve *reports* to Adam.
Due to our fallen nature, they believe we need to focus on
order. Pre-Fall people are concerned more with freedom.

So how do well-intended believers on both sides of this
issue get beyond the theological wars that don't seem to be
getting us anywhere? Perhaps we can start by trying to understand some of the underlying forces—specifically our views
of sin and power—that have a more profound impact on our
beliefs than we generally realize.

The Sin of Indifference

During the Middle Ages, the Roman Catholic Church developed a dogma regarding sin, which categorized sins as either "mortal" or "venial." Because mortal sins were more serious and committed deliberately, they required more elaborate penance than venial sins. During the Reformation, Protestants rejected these classifications. Even today, evangelicals loudly proclaim that Jesus died for all of our sins and there is nothing we can do to earn his forgiveness, an assertion I happen to believe as well.

Meanwhile, evangelicals continue to give Catholics theological grief over these categories of sin. This could be written off as an exercise in religious playground bullying if it were not for the fact that evangelicals have some major blind spots.

After thirty-five years in evangelicalism, I've learned which sins matter most.

In my observation, evangelicals have created their own hierarchy of sin, which looks something like this:

Evangelical level-one sins (what Catholics call mortal sins):

- Murder
- Rape
- Abortion
- Premarital sex
- Homosexuality
- Adultery

Evangelical level-two sins (what Catholics call venial sins):

- Divorce
- Anger
- Lust
- Pornography
- Gossip
- Viewing R-rated movies
- Voting Democrat

Evangelical level-three sins (a.k.a. "not that big of a deal"):

- Rudeness
- Gluttony
- Consumerism
- Large church buildings

Sins evangelicals historically haven't thought much about (a.k.a. systemic sins):

- Sexism
- Racism
- Disregard for the environment
- Greed
- Politicization of Christianity

Although you might quibble with my rankings, I'm confident in my assertion that systemic sins are rarely talked about in our churches. In fact, in the first twenty-five years after I came to Christ, I never heard (or gave) one sermon on social justice or systemic sin. All I heard and preached about were the evils of personal sin (levels one to three).

In general, evangelicals have been taught that people should pull themselves up by their own bootstraps, which might say more about the influence the cult of American individualism has had on our thinking than it does about our understanding of the Bible. If we place too high a value on self-sufficiency, we are likely to overlook the most vulnerable among us. That may be why, for most of its history, evangelicalism tended to spiritualize the parts of the Bible that take systemic sin seriously, such as the Sermon on the Mount and the parable of the sheep and goats. Fortunately, that view is beginning to shift.

While completing my doctoral studies at Bakke Graduate University, I learned about systemic sin for the first time, and it changed the way I read the Bible. I had the privilege of traveling with the school's namesake, Dr. Ray Bakke, and serving as his teaching assistant in a class on church history. Ray's life has been a model of what it looks like to combat systemic sin. He's a veteran of evangelicalism who spent thirty years pastoring a small church in inner-city Chicago. During that time he and his wife adopted African American children.

While ministering in the inner city, Bakke learned to work shoulder to shoulder in advancing the gospel with all sorts of people. In his book *A Theology as Big as the City*, Bakke reflects on how God worked through Esther, Nehemiah, and Ezra to prepare the exiled Jews to return to their homeland and then comments on what that might mean for male and female Christians today:

> This partnership also reminds us that both men and women are needed on the team. . . . Some American city communities are so violent that only women will be safe and effective as evangelists, pastors, and church planters. Their vulnerability is their power in many emasculated, gang-ridden neighborhoods. I've also seen this pattern in repeated visits to places like Beirut and Belfast over the years. The men are dead or not trusted. The women are building God's church.[2]

Power Grab

I've worked on this book for almost three years. During that time I've talked with, listened to, and read comments from hundreds of women. I told my wife, "Sometimes I feel like I am swimming in estrogen." In fact, when women heard about this project, they enthusiastically put forward numerous topics for me to consider—everything from patriarchalism, egalitarianism, and complementarianism to misogyny and social justice. While I'm certainly familiar with and sympathetic to all of these topics, what really interested me was trying to understand the underlying issue that fuels and informs this debate. Where is all the heat coming from? Why is this issue so personal for so many men and women?

I didn't decide to follow Jesus in order to get to heaven, escape hell, or be holy or right.

I accepted Jesus' invitation to join his movement for one simple reason: Jesus is the freest person who ever lived, and I want to be free.

What made Jesus free is that he didn't *need* power.

What makes us slaves is that we do.

I chose not to address directly the issues my women friends suggested because, as I see it, they're symptoms— important symptoms, but symptoms nonetheless. Since this is the only book I anticipate ever writing on this topic, I want to focus on the key issue that I think informs not only the gender wars but also the racial, economic, and political wars.

The core problem, I'm convinced, is power—how we get it, manage it, and give it away. Power is not political; it's primal. Our desire for power is visceral and cannot be reasoned with. It leaves us only two options: power has to be either taken or given.

When *USA Today* examined the impact of male mentors on women, they discussed a report from Catalyst, an organization dedicated to the advancement of women in business, which studied the influence of male mentors on the careers of women. Following is one of the report's findings:

Men who impeded or who were indifferent to the progress of women viewed the workplace as a zero-sum game where promotions of women came at the expense of men. Catalyst found that if there is one thing that stands out among male champions of women, it is a strong sense of fairness.[3]

Jesus is the leader of a movement whose central organizing feature is the act of giving power away, particularly to those who lack it. Those who claim him as Lord, Savior, and leader have committed themselves to this way of life.

Based on my reading of the Gospels, I think it's clear that Jesus wants women to have as much power as men. (He wants the same for people suffering from racial, political, and economic discrimination.) How he wants them to go about getting that power, however, is another story.

The question for me, then, is this: have we become so conformed to the world that we can no longer be transformed by Jesus?

What would happen if in obedience to the tradition of our Master we focused more energy on giving power away than on hoarding it for ourselves?

While I personally would support an affirmative action program for women in the church, in the final analysis we can't legislate love. And since followers of Jesus have signed up for the love game, if we violate that value on the way to winning, we will end up losing. Again, in the spirit of our Master who flipped the tables in the Temple on their tops, I'm ready to protest the abuse and misuse of power, but not at the expense of violating the rule of our Master who said we are to love our neighbors and even our enemies.

As I see it, if women want power, they'll need to hew more closely to what Jesus said in Matthew 10:16 (NLT): "I am sending you out as sheep among wolves. So be as shrewd as snakes and harmless as doves." For the most part, women have the "innocent as doves" piece completely dialed in. What they need to figure out now is what being "shrewd as snakes" looks like. For women, this may mean becoming fierce pragmatists.

In this book you've read the stories of women who have boldly and thoughtfully moved forward in pursuit of God's calling on their lives. I've profiled other women who have found ways to collaborate with men who are motivated to help them. And I believe there are several steps that leaders of both genders within the church can take to help all women exercise their influence.

What Now?

Let's face it—when it comes to systemic sins, inertia holds off change as long as possible. Consequently, most of us will only be able to take baby steps. As I conclude, I'd like to offer some final ideas to consider if you're interested in opening the path of influence for women in your church.

Level the playing field. In his book *Outliers*, Malcolm Gladwell talks about the Matthew Effect, an idea based on

Matthew 25:29: "For everyone who has will be given more, and he will have an abundance. Whoever does not have, even what he has will be taken from him."

Gladwell argues that talent has far less to do with one's level of success than the circumstances into which the person is born. For example, in researching the backgrounds of all the players on the successful 2007 Czech junior hockey team, Gladwell discovered that for the most part all the players were born between January and August, giving them what sociologists call an "accumulative advantage" over those born in the last quarter of the year. As a result, he says, "Those who are successful . . . are most likely to be given the kinds of special opportunities that lead to further success."[4] What if we acted on his suggestion to rewrite the rules so that *all talented people can have an opportunity to make the highest and best use of their gifts?*

What if we provided rules that leveled the playing field and made it easier for women to pursue influence and leadership, wherever their talent takes them? One can dream, but for the time being, most evangelical women are like the Czech players who happened to be born in the last three months of the year—destined to sit and watch, in this case simply because they were born the wrong gender.

Look for opportunities to champion women. In chapter 2, I talked about my friendship with Dr. Rose Madrid-Swetman. I also acknowledged that some of my interest in seeing her succeed was fueled by the lack of opportunity my own mother experienced as a single mom raising four kids alone. I've discovered that there are a number of men like me who are motivated to help women move into whatever levels of influence and leadership they desire. Interestingly, we all share one constant: each of us has had a strong female influence, whether from our mothers, our wives, or our daughters.

The *USA Today* article "Often, Men Help Women Get to the Corner Office" illustrates how critical a male's support has been to women in the executive suite. When the newspaper asked female CEOs to name the mentor who had contributed the most to their careers, thirty-three of the thirty-four respondents identified a man.

> One reason the path to success for some women almost always leads through men may be the sheer matter of numbers: There are only *29 Fortune 1,000 companies with a female CEO* and not enough other women in very high-ranking positions to do the mentoring.

USA Today discovered something interesting when it profiled the men whom the female executives identified as their mentors: "What do these mentors have in common? . . . One thread appears to be that they often have a daughter. Others have had a strong female influence in their lives." In fact, Catalyst reported that 83 percent of the men they identified as champions had at least one daughter. When *USA Today* asked top corporate women if their key male mentors had a daughter, 70 percent said yes.[5]

Interestingly, Presidents Barack Obama, George W. Bush, and Bill Clinton appear to support this connection as well. Consider this: "Of the 40 women who were appointed by U.S. presidents to Cabinet posts, 26 were appointed by the last three presidents—*all of whom have daughters and no sons*."[6]

Systemic changes are more important than symbolic gestures. When President Obama stood on the stage in Chicago to accept the nomination to be the Democratic candidate for president of the United States, it was a palpably symbolic moment for African Americans. Black people have gotten used to the system working against them, so when a black man took the stage, looked them in the eye, and uttered those powerful words, "Yes, we can," it *really mattered*. Suddenly those who had long been denied power could envision themselves being treated fairly in America.

This wasn't Snoop Dogg rapping, Morgan Freeman acting, or Michael Jordan dunking. This was even bigger than Oprah. In this symbolic act, the systemic sin of racism was attacked at the highest level of power, and African Americans felt it in a way white people would never be able to.

Nevertheless, when it comes to obliterating racism, the most generous thing you can say about the election of President Obama is, "It's a start—maybe."

Ashleigh Shelby Rosette, assistant professor of management in Duke's Fuqua School of Business, conducts research on how minorities in America are perceived in various leadership positions. She noted,

> Sometimes people say, "Well, we have Obama as president now; those perceptions should go away." But if I ask what's the race of the next president going to be, you're probably going to say, "White." Because we only have one [black president], and one doesn't change the perception. *If you want to change perceptions, you have to change the numbers.* Once the numbers change, the perceptions will follow.

As far as women pulling themselves up by their bootstraps, Rosette says:

> We'd like to say, "Just do your best and it's always going to be recognized," but unfortunately that's not the case. Until the numbers are there at the top echelons, you have to recognize things that you're going to have to negotiate. Who the audience is may affect which behaviors you emphasize, because there are different standards for women as they progress up the ladder.[7]

Translation: Until the number of women elders, senior pastors, and denominational leaders increases, the perception that they are not able to lead will persist. Which begs the question, how will women gain access to these levels of influence? The answer? They'll have to go through, over, around, or arm in arm with men.

I remember hearing a National Public Radio interview with one of the first women parliamentarians in Afghanistan. She explained that when she suggested that the government of Afghanistan begin tracking the number of women who currently serve in the parliament and other political offices, she was rebuffed by her male colleagues. She was told "that would be too difficult for us to track," apparently meaning men in Afghanistan don't know how to count heads.

She responded, "If we don't count, we will never have the data to demonstrate whether or not we are keeping our word to the nation that women will be treated with equality in our country."

Likewise, if church leaders and influencers do not track our progress in ensuring women are able to use their giftedness and influence in the church, we will make little progress. If you have a competent female leader in your congregation whom you'd like to invite to assume a significant role, don't assume that her involvement alone will change things. Your church will need to work consciously toward a system that encourages both men and women to use their particular gifts and influence in the way God has called them.

Amerigo Vespucci, the Bible, and Mental Maps

The maps we use are subjective—they're drawings of how explorers "see" their world, city, or neighborhood. Their maps represent how they think we should see the world. Consequently, maps at times leave out details their creators simply didn't know about.

This was particularly evident when the New World was being discovered. It was only five hundred years ago that Amerigo Vespucci and his companions mapped the coast of South America. They made it at least as far south as present-day Rio de Janeiro, and possibly even farther. For Vespucci this was a whole new landmass. Vespucci was hoping to find Asia, but accidentally bumped into South America.

After returning to Lisbon, Vespucci wrote that the landmasses they explored were much larger than they had anticipated, differed in shape from the Asian continent of Ptolemy's *Geographia*, and were completely unlike the Far Eastern civilization described in *The Travels of Marco Polo*. As a result, he asserted that he and his men must have stumbled upon a New World.

This is the map that emerged from their exploration. Essentially the drawing represents their best guess as to what the east coast of much of the Americas was like. Given that they had no accurate way to measure longitude and no satellite images, it's amazing how accurately the coastline is portrayed. However, they had no idea what they had actually discovered. The true scope of that would have to wait for future explorers like Magellan, Balboa, and Lewis and Clark.

For two thousand years Christianity has been working off the mental maps that were created by our own explorers (many of whom lived during the same era as Vespucci). Is it

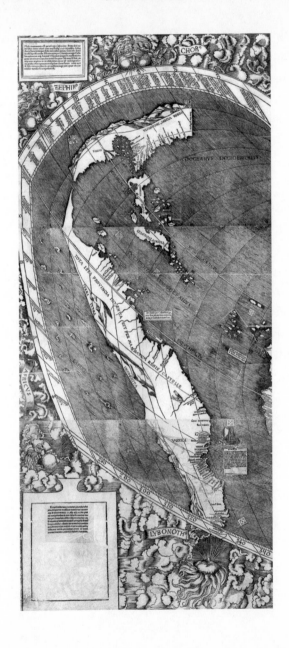

possible that, similar to Vespucci's map, some of the maps we've inherited are also wrong—limited by the perceptions of their creators, *including how God views women?*

Forgive me for asking this, but what if Jesus isn't coming back anytime soon?

What if this first two thousand years was just the opening act and the church's best days are ahead? (I think I hear a lot of cheers coming from Gen Ys right now.)

What Vespucci discovered and attempted to map for his countrymen was groundbreaking *and also wrong.*

What if like Vespucci's map, our perception of God's heart is far too narrow?

What if his heart is wider and higher than we've been taught to imagine?

What if God's ways really aren't our ways?

Maybe Jesus can help us with that.

Let us pray.

Acknowledgments

Here are the women who have formed, influenced, impacted, and provoked me into becoming a better person.

My wife, Barbara; my daughters, Sarah and Judah; my daughter-in-law Kelli Henderson; my mother, Jacqueline Wallace; my sister, Leigh, and her daughters; and my sisters-in-law Kathy MacKintosh and Susie Ellis and their daughters. My former comrades-in-arms: Ollie Smith, Kandy Rettig, Linda Brockway, Jeannette Case, Maureen Burke, Carol Allard, Val O'Neil, Chris McDaniels, Renee Fox, Jacki Dunlap, Mary McKinney, Sarita Fernandes, Blessi Kumar, Elizabeth Di Candilo, and Barbro Askew. The women I sang with: Jessica Ketola, Joanna Brantley, and Cherese Sutton. The pastors I respect: Julie Clark, Deborah Loyd, Rose Madrid-Swetman, Debbie Hunter, Charlotte Baker, Kathy Escobar, Kelly Bean, Molly DuQue, Julie Clark, Dawn Oas, Sheila Cherian, Lisa Domke, and Grace McLaren.

The educators who have influenced me include Mary Kate Morse, Shirley Akers, Judy Melton, Molly Kenzler, and

Sheila Bartlett. My agent, Esther Fedorkevich; my publisher (and the person who came up with the very creative title of this book), Jan Long Harris; and my editor, Kim Miller. The women who are married to my close colleagues: Cote Soerens, Tina Smith, Sandy Siever, Anne Shantz, and Sara Spinks. The women I've worked shoulder to shoulder with in leadership, church planting, movement planting, and Kingdom advancing: Pam Sardar, Julie Nagel, Vicki Baird, Darci Rubart, Leigh Buchan, Diane Ellis, Geneva Vollrath, Mary Schaller, Elizabeth Chapin, Sharon Karns, Sharon Richards, Nancy Short, Lani Faith, Lisa Wellington, and the Circus Sisters, Sister Dorothy Fabritze and Sister Bernard Overkamp.

Finally, I want to acknowledge four other women who have had profound influence on my life: Helen Mildenhall, who taught me about dialogue; Christine Wicker, a wonderful writer and courageously open person; Kris Hoots Thomas, my social media coach and great friend; and Elaine Hansen, my coworker who's stuck with me through thick and thin. Pam Hogeweide was particularly helpful to me as I wrote the book. In fact, she recounted Denie Tackett's story to me and was instrumental in connecting me with a number of other women for this project.

Without the help of all these women (and many more), I would have had nothing to say on this topic.

Selected Barna Group Survey Data on Women and the Church

THIS APPENDIX PRESENTS some of the overall findings from a nationwide random survey of females, eighteen years of age or older, who consider themselves to be Christian and who attend Christian church services. The survey includes responses from 603 such women randomly sampled from across the forty-eight continental states. The outcomes are based upon telephone interviews conducted by The Barna Group in April 2010. The maximum margin of sampling error associated with the aggregate sample is ±4.1 percentage points at the 95 percent confidence level. Note that for some questions the responses shown do not total 100 percent, either because of rounding or because the "don't know" response is not shown. In some questions the responses add up to more than 100 percent because multiple responses were allowed for, as indicated by the notation after the question (multiple responses allowed).

1. I'd like to know more about how you describe yourself. I'm going to read a list of descriptions and would like you to tell me if each of these adjectives is a very accurate, somewhat accurate, or not too accurate description of you.

	Very	Somewhat	Not Too
a leader	36%	46%	18%
a servant	49%	32%	15%
deeply spiritual	65%	29%	5%
mature in your faith	74%	24%	2%

The following question was asked only if the respondent called herself a leader in the first question:

2. You mentioned that you are a leader. In what settings or in what type of activities do you provide leadership? (Note: response options were not read to respondents; multiple responses were allowed.)

At a church 52%
On the job 31%
Parenting/in home/with family 29%
In the community/neighborhood 28%
At a school 18%
At a nonprofit/community organization 13%

3. As you examine your spiritual life, is there anything you do on purpose as your way of intentionally serving God? (Note: response options were not read to respondents; multiple responses were allowed.)

Pray for others 46%
Encourage people 24%
Help needy/disadvantaged/homeless people 24%

Talk about Jesus/gospel with people 23%
Volunteer at church 21%
Donate money to religious causes 17%
No, no intentional service 13%
Volunteer at a nonprofit/service organization 9%
Provide leadership to a group 8%
Teach a religious class 8%

4. Overall, do you think you are *capable* of doing more to serve God than you are currently doing?

Yes 83%

The following question was asked only if the respondent answered yes to question 4.

5. Overall, do you think you *should be* doing more to serve God than you are currently doing?

Yes 87%

6. What prevents you or holds you back from doing more to serve God? (Note: response options were not read to respondents; multiple responses were allowed.)

Lack of opportunities; gender restrictions; women not allowed 27%
Not sure what to do 12%
No time; too busy 11%
Have not thought about it much 7%
Laziness; selfishness 7%
Health restrictions; age 6%
No resources 5%
Fear of failure 4%
Family obligations 3%
No training/preparation 3%
Not good enough at anything 2%

7. How similar is your church's perspective on the role
   of women in ministry with your perspective?

   Almost identical 27%
   Very similar 34%
   Somewhat similar 23%
   Not too similar 6%
   Almost completely different 5%
   Don't know 4%

8. Think about the roles that you fill in your church.
   Please tell me if the following words accurately
   describe how you feel about serving in your
   church: you are resigned to their expectations.
   Does that describe your feelings accurately
   or not?

   Yes 31%
   No 59%
   Don't know 10%

9. Are there any types of leadership activities or
   roles in your church that are not currently
   open or available to women, strictly because of
   their gender? (Note: response options were not
   read to respondents; multiple responses were
   allowed.)

   Yes—pastoral staff 23%
   Yes—elders/deacons/trustees/vestry/board 11%
   Yes—teaching men 3%
   Yes—administrative staff 3%
   Yes—teaching (anyone—men, women, children) 2%
   Yes—other roles 1%

10. As far as you know, what are the main reasons why women are not allowed to fill some of those leadership roles or positions? (Note: response options were not read to respondents; multiple responses were allowed.)

Biblical principles 64%
Believe women are not as capable 4%
Tradition/history 4%
Church doctrine/church rules 3%
Women are not strong/tough enough 3%
Women lack the same level of training 2%

11. If you were given an open invitation to exercise a greater degree of leadership in your church, how likely would you be to invest more of your time and energy in leading in your church? Would you . . .

Definitely do so 16%
Probably do so 40%
Probably not do so 33%
Definitely not do so 10%
Don't know 2%

12. Men hold many different roles in society and have a variety of opinions about women serving in leadership roles. I'm going to mention some of those male roles and would like to know how supportive you feel the men who hold those positions are of allowing women to provide leadership in any role within your church.

How supportive is this person of allowing women to lead?

Position	Completely	Highly	Somewhat	Not Too	Not At All	Don't Know
your senior pastor	42%	26%	15%	4%	6%	6%
your husband	41%	22%	19%	4%	9%	6%
the men on the board of elders	31%	23%	23%	3%	7%	14%

13. To change our focus a bit, I'm going to read some statements to you about women leading in the local church. Please listen carefully to each statement and then tell me if, based on your personal experience at your church, you agree or disagree with the statement. Do you agree/disagree somewhat or strongly?

Statement	Agree Strongly	Agree Somewhat	Disagree Somewhat	Disagree Strongly	Don't Know
your church provides women with the same degree of leadership opportunities that Jesus would give them	55%	26%	6%	7%	6%
you can tell by its actions that your church values the leadership of women as much as it values the leadership of men	55%	27%	9%	6%	3%
you have more opportunities to lead outside of your church than you do within your church	22%	19%	22%	29%	7%
you believe that most of the men in your church would prefer that women have more leadership opportunities in your church	17%	27%	26%	17%	14%

Statement	Agree Strongly	Agree Somewhat	Disagree Somewhat	Disagree Strongly	Don't Know
you would be more active in your church if you had more opportunities to use your leadership abilities there	12%	19%	27%	38%	5%
you believe that the Bible prohibits women from being leaders in your church	10%	9%	23%	53%	6%

Endnotes

FOREWORD

1. The biblical study that led to this conclusion is captured in *Beyond Sex Roles*, a book by former Wheaton College professor and Willow Creek elder, Dr. Gilbert Bilezikian.

2. Jesse Ellison, "Where Women Are Winning, *Newsweek*, September 18, 2011.

AUTHOR'S NOTE

1. In November 2010, Yoida Full Gospel Church released twenty satellite congregations to become independent, which resulted in a drop of over 300,000 people from its membership rolls. See http://www.charismamag .com/index.php/news-old/29486-pruning-the-worlds-largest-church; see also"O Come All Ye Faithful," *The Economist*, November 1, 2007, http://www.economist.com/node/10015239?story_id=10015239&CFID =25385374.

2. The Barna Group, "Women Are the Backbone of the Christian Congregations in America," March 6, 2000.

3. Reggie McNeal, *The Present Future* (San Francisco: Jossey-Bass, 2003), 3–4; based on George Barna's State of the Church 2002. Note: George Barna defines the "unchurched" as not having attended a Christian church service, other than for a holiday service, such as Christmas or Easter, or for special events such as a wedding or funeral, at any time in the past six months.

4. Albert L. Winseman, "How Many Americans Are 'Unchurched'?" Gallup, October 11, 2005, http://www.gallup.com/poll/19129/how-many -americans-unchurched.aspx.

5. Steve Smith, "Study Tracks Church Attendance Trends," press release, University of Nebraska–Lincoln, April 15, 2010, http://scarlet.unl .edu/?p=8242.

6. I use the word *influence* because it includes *but is not limited to* "leadership." Jesus treated women like Mary Magdalene and the Samaritan woman in John 4 not only with honor but also with intellectual respect. He didn't talk down to them or patronize them. He asked them to do

difficult things and to use their influence to help others. He approached them in a way that demonstrated his belief that they were as spiritually competent as any men he interacted with.

I found it interesting to discover that denominations (whether liberal or conservative) that officially provide women an open door to the highest levels of influence often unofficially block them from walking through that same door. For more on this, be sure to read my interview with Amy Snow in chapter 9.

CHAPTER 1: THE THREE FACES OF RESIGNATION

1. The Barna Group, "Do Americans Change Faiths?" August 16, 2010, http://www.barna.org/faith-spirituality/412-do-americans-change-faiths.
2. Daniel Pink, *A Whole New Mind* (New York: Berkley, 2006), 103.
3. Anne Lamott, quoting her priest friend Tom in *Bird by Bird* (New York: Anchor Books, 1994), 21–22.
4. When conducting surveys, Barna defines Born-Again Christians as those people who say they have made "a personal commitment to Jesus Christ that is still important in their life today" and who also indicate they believe that when they die they will go to heaven because they have confessed their sins and accepted Jesus Christ as their Savior. Respondents are not asked to describe themselves as "born again." Being classified as "born again" is not dependent upon church or denominational affiliation or involvement.

    About 63 percent of the women who took part in the Barna research study for this book were classified as Born Again.

CHAPTER 2: WHY IT MATTERS

1. *Outsiders* is the term I use for the people Jesus misses most—those formerly known as lost, the unsaved, non-Christians, unredeemed, etc. It correctly identifies the us/them divide we have created in our understanding of who's in and who's out.
2. As reported in "Senior Class Day" in the *Yale Bulletin & Calendar*, vol. 31, no. 31 (June 6, 2003), http://www.yale.edu/opa/arc-ybc/v31.n31 /story104.html.

CHAPTER 3: SUBMITTED

1. Hanna Rosin, "The End of Men," *The Atlantic*, July/August 2010.
2. The term *spiritual covering* comes out of a biblical interpretation that says each of us needs another person to whom we are accountable and submitted. Proponents believe women, in particular, need a man as a covering. Usually this is their husband, but in the most conservative circles this injunction

includes even unmarried women. According to this theory, the person above us serves not only as an accountability partner but also (for those who are properly submitted) protection from Satan and deception.

CHAPTER 4: TALL MEN DON'T, BUT I DO

1. Dan Brennan, *Sacred Unions, Sacred Passions* (Elgin, IL: Faith Dance, 2010).
2. "For this reason, and because of the angels, the woman ought to have a sign of authority on her head. In the Lord, however, woman is not independent of man, nor is man independent of woman. For as woman came from man, so also man is born of woman. But everything comes from God. Judge for yourselves: Is it proper for a woman to pray to God with her head uncovered?" (1 Corinthians 11:10-13)
3. James Davison Hunter, *To Change the World* (New York: Oxford, 2010), 12.
4. See my book *The Outsider Interviews* (Grand Rapids, MI: Baker Publishing, 2010), which I cowrote with Todd Hunter and Craig Spinks.

CHAPTER 5: YOUR LIFE WILL NEVER BE THE SAME

1. Lawrence A. Greenfeld et al., "Violence by Intimates," US Department of Justice, March 1998, http://bjs.ojp.usdoj.gov/content/pub/pdf/vi.pdf; Karen Scott Collins et al., "Health Concerns across a Woman's Lifespan," The Commonwealth Fund, May 5, 1999, http://www.commonwealth fund.org/Content/Publications/Fund-Reports/1999/May/Health -Concerns-Across-a-Womans-Lifespan--The-Commonwealth-Fund -1998-Survey-of-Womens-Health.aspx.

CHAPTER 7: I WONDER WHAT WOULD HAVE HAPPENED

1. When it comes to women and influence, the Roman Catholic Church ends up exactly where conservative evangelicals do, although they arrive there using a different rationale. Evangelicals quote specific passages in the Bible, but Catholics refer to history or what they call "tradition," which they feel is equal to the Bible. Their tradition tells them that the priesthood is reserved for men only. They do, however, continue to practice the evangelical tradition of using women to do the work.

CHAPTER 9: YOU DON'T ALWAYS GET WHAT YOU WANT

1. While still making up a small percentage of the total number of senior pastors, more women are leading churches today than in past decades. The Barna Group reports the percentage of female senior pastors increased from 5 percent to 10 percent between 1999 and 2009. For more details, see "Number of Female Senior Pastors in Protestant Churches Doubles in Past Decade," http://www.barna.org/barna-update

/article/17-leadership/304-number-of-female-senior-pastors-in-protestant
-churches-doubles-in-past-decade.

2. Genesis 5:2, KJV, italics added.

CHAPTER 10: EATING INTO THE PRINCIPAL

1. Calvin Miller, "The Slow, Slow Art of Urgency for Women in Ministry" (sermon, Woman's Missionary Union annual meeting, Atlanta, June 13, 1999), http://www.christianethicstoday.com/cetart/index.cfm?fuseaction =Articles.main&ArtID=659.

2. Thanks to my friend Peter Block, consultant and author of *Community* (San Francisco: Berrett-Koehler Publishers, 2008), for this insight.

3. When I searched the words *egalitarian* and *complementarian* at Google, a few of the resources that came up were: *Manly Dominion and Womanly Dominion* by Mark Chanski; *Equal Yet Different* by Alexander Strauch; *Man and Woman, One in Christ* by Philip B. Payne; *Beyond Sex Roles* by Gilbert Bilezikian; *How I Changed My Mind about Women in Leadership*, ed. Alan F. Johnson; *Two Views on Women in Ministry*, ed. James R. Beck and Craig L. Blomberg; and *Men and Women in the Church* by Sarah Sumner.

CHAPTER 11: SHE LEFT THE HOMESCHOOL CHURCH

1. Clay Shirky, *Here Comes Everybody: The Power of Organizing without Organizations* (New York: Penguin, 2008), 303.

CHAPTER 12: WHOSE JESUS SHOULD I FOLLOW?

1. Helen blogs at www.mildenhall.net.

CHAPTER 13: CHANGE A METAPHOR, CHANGE A LIFE

1. Susan Hall, "My Journey to Feminism," *Christian Feminism Today* 32, no. 4, winter 2009, http://www.eewc.com/CFT/v32n4a1.htm.

CHAPTER 14: YOU DON'T NEED PERMISSION

1. Malcolm Gladwell, *Outliers: The Story of Success* (New York: Little, Brown, and Co., 2008), 204–209. *Power distance index* is one of five differentials in the cultural dimensions theory, a systematic framework developed by Dutch social psychologist Geert Hofstede to assess and differentiate national cultures.

CHAPTER 19: PRESIDENT, SURE! PASTOR, SHHH!

1. On May 2, 2010, Pastor Larry Kroon gave a message in which he explained Wasilla Bible Church's application of 1 Timothy 2:12, which reads, "I don't allow a woman to teach or exercise authority over a man." He said, "So as a

congregation here, our practice is that we do not have women on our elder board. That isn't an issue of whether they're superior or inferior, or anything like that. It's just simply applying this passage. And secondly, we don't have them filling our pastoral preaching role either, in other words teaching from the pulpit on Sunday mornings. That's the way we've chosen to apply this passage." See http://wasillabible.org/sermon_files/2010_Transcripts/The%20Church3-The%20Practical.pdf.

2. The Nashville-based United Methodist Church has a total of 44,842 clergy, and about 10,000—23 percent—are female. Of the denomination's largest churches, just 85 are led by women, compared to 1,082 men in such positions. "Methodist Women Seek to Crack 'Stained-Glass Ceiling,'" *USA Today*, January 22, 2009, http://www.usatoday.com/news/religion/2009-01-22-methodist-women_N.htm.

3. The Barna Group, "Americans Are Exploring New Ways of Experiencing God," June 8, 2009, http://www.barna.org/barna-update/article/12-faith spirituality/270-americans-are-exploring-new-ways-of-experiencing-god.

4. The Barna Group, "Who Is Active in 'Group' Expressions of Faith?" Barna Study Examines Small Groups, Sunday School, and House Churches," June 28, 2010, http://www.barna.org/faith-spirituality/400-who-is-active -in-group-expressions-of-faith-barna-study-examines-small-groups-sunday -school-and-house-churches.

5. Ibid.

6. The Barna Group, "Number of Female Senior Pastors in Protestant Churches Doubles in Past Decade," 2009, http://www.barna.org/barna -update/article/17-leadership/304-number-of-female-senior-pastors-in -protestant-churches-doubles-in-past-decade.

7. Ibid.

8. Rosin, "The End of Men."

9. Ibid.

10. Ibid.

11. Ibid.

12. Sharon Vosmek, "Closing the Venture Capital Gender Gap," *Bloomberg BusinessWeek*, June 24, 2010.

13. Ibid.

14. Martha M. Lauzen, "The Celluloid Ceiling: Behind-the-Scenes Employment of Women on the Top 250 Films of 2009," 2010, http://womenintvfilm.sdsu.edu/files/2009_Celluloid_Ceiling.pdf.

15. Sheri R. Benvenuti, "Pentecostal Women in Ministry: Where Do We Go from Here?" *Cyberjournal for Pentecostal-Charismatic Research*, January 1997, http://www.pctii.org/cyberj/cyberj1/ben.html.

16. Ibid.

17. Christian NewsWire, "The Foursquare Church Appoints Woman as General Supervisor," http://www.christiannewswire.com/news/8200114246.html.

18. Ibid.

19. Barna, "Americans Are Exploring New Ways of Experiencing God."

20. To their credit, the Foursquare denomination recently made a significant change by appointing Rev. Tammy Dunahoo to the office of general supervisor (See note 17).

21. Christopher Landau, "Will South Korea become Christian?" *BBC News,* October 26, 2009, http://news.bbc.co.uk/2/hi/8322072.stm.

22. "David Yonggi Cho," *Wikipedia,* http://en.wikipedia.org/wiki /David_Yonggi_Cho.

23. "Breakfast with David Yonggi Cho and Rick Warren," *Pastors.com,* 2001, http://webmailimages.pastors.com/article.asp?ArtID=578.

24. Andy Butcher, "Don't Be Afraid to Empower Women," *Beliefnet,* http://www .beliefnet.com/Faiths/2000/07/Dont-Be-Afraid-To-Empower-Women.aspx. Reprinted by *Beliefnet* with permission from Charisma News Service.

25. Rosin, "The End of Men."

26. Brennan, *Sacred Unions, Sacred Passions,* 100.

27. Catherine Mowry LaCugna, *God for Us: The Trinity and Christian Life* (New York: HarperOne, 1991), 194.

CHAPTER 20: WHEN ONLY A WOMAN WILL DO

1. Ronald E. Keener, "Churches Lose Strength When Women Are Excluded in Leadership," *ChurchExecutive.com,* July 1, 2010, http://churchexecutive .com/archives/churches-lose-strength-when-women-are-excluded-in -leadership. (Article cited is an interview with Shaunti Feldhahn, author of *The Male Factor* [Multnomah, 2009]).

2. Ray Bakke, *A Theology as Big as the City* (Downers Grove, IL: InterVarsity Press, 1997), 111.

3. Del Jones, "Often, Men Help Women Get to the Corner Office," *USA Today,* August 5, 2009, http://www.usatoday.com/money/companies /management/2009-08-04-female-executives-male-mentors_N.htm.

4. Malcolm Gladwell, *Outliers* (New York: Little, Brown and Company, 2008), 30.

5. Jones, "Often, Men Help Women Get to the Corner Office."

6. Ibid., italics mine.

7. "Ashleigh Shelby Rosette: The Feminization of Management," *Faith & Leadership,* June 22, 2010, http://www.faithandleadership.com/node /1511?page=full&print=true.

Online Discussion *guide*

Take *your* TYNDALE READING EXPERIENCE *to the* NEXT LEVEL

A FREE discussion guide for this book is available at bookclubhub.net, perfect for sparking conversations in your book group or for digging deeper into the text on your own.

www.bookclubhub.net

You'll also find free discussion guides for other Tyndale books, e-newsletters, e-mail devotionals, virtual book tours, and more!

Barna Books encourage and resource committed believers seeking lives of vibrant faith—and call the church to a new understanding of what it means to be the Church.

For more information, visit www.tyndale.com/barnabooks.

BARNA

CP0309

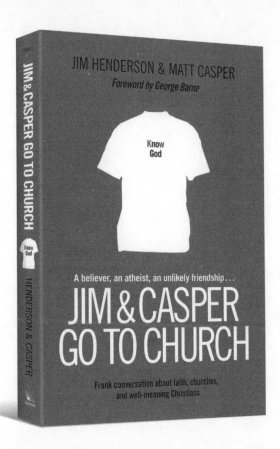

JIM HENDERSON & MATT CASPER

Foreword by George Barna

Know
God

A believer, an atheist, an unlikely friendship...

JIM & CASPER GO TO CHURCH

Frank conversation about faith, churches,
and well-meaning Christians

What would an atheist think about Jesus after visiting your church?

Jim Henderson decided that the best way to find out was to ask! So he recruited an atheist—Matt Casper—to visit twelve leading churches with him and give the "first impression" perspective of a non-believer. Follow along with Jim and Casper on their visits, and eavesdrop as they discuss what they found. Their articulate, sometimes humorous, and always insightful dialogue offers Christians a new view of an environment where we've become overly comfortable: the church.

ISBN 978-1-4143-5858-1